Catherine L'Ecuyer is Canadian, now living in Barcelona with her four children. She holds a law degree, has an MBA, an Official European Master of Research and a Doctorate in Education and Psychology. The Swiss journal *Frontiers in Human Neuroscience* published her article "The Wonder Approach to learning", which converted her thesis into a new education hypothesis/theory. She received the 2015 Pajarita Award from the Spanish Association of Toy Manufacturers for "promoting a culture of play in the media", and was invited to speak to the Education Commission of the Congress of Deputies of Spain and at the 2019 European Education Summit organised by the European Commission. She has served as a consultant to the Spanish government regarding the use of digital technology by minors, to the government of the state of Puebla in Mexico concerning preschool reform, and has participated in a report for the Cerlac (UNESCO) on the use of digital media in childhood.

Initially published in Spain (25th ed.), *The Wonder Approach* has been published in eight languages and is available in more than sixty countries. She has also published *Educar en la realidad* (9th ed.), on the use of digital media in childhood and adolescence. A video interview she did as part of *Aprendemos Juntos* (BBVA-El País) received over 10 million views in the course of a few months and has won the Google YouTube Ads Leaderboard award for being the third most creative advertising video on YouTube. A sought-after international speaker, she currently collaborates with the Mind-Brain Group of the University of Navarra and is a columnist for *El País*, one of the most-read newspapers in Spanish.

Contact: agenda@catherinelecuyer.com
Web: www.catherinelecuyer-eng.com

CATHERINE L'ECUYER

The Wonder Approach

Rescuing Children's Innate Desire to Learn

ROBINSON

ROBINSON

First published in Spain in 2012 by Plataforma

This English edition published in Great Britain in 2019 by Robinson

Translation by Andrew Sheedy
Co-translation by Catherine L'Ecuyer

A CIP catalogue record for this book is available from the British Library

ISBN: 978-1-47214-385-3

Typeset in Times by Initial Typesetting Services, Edinburgh
Printed and bound in Great Britain by Clays Ltd, Elcograf S.p.A.

Papers used by Robinson are from well-managed forests
and other responsible sources

Robinson
An imprint of
Little, Brown Book Group
Carmelite House
50 Victoria Embankment
London EC4Y 0DZ

An Hachette UK Company
www.hachette.co.uk

www.littlebrown.co.uk

For Domingo, for sharing with me his sensitivity for the natural laws of childhood, helping me find meaning in what I now consider the best job in the world: being a mother.

*When we are very young children we do not
need fairy tales: we only need tales. Mere life
is interesting enough. A child of seven is excited
by being told that Tommy opened a door and saw
a dragon. But a child of three is excited by being
told that Tommy opened a door.*

G. K. Chesterton

Contents

Part III
Conclusion

Introduction

Calm children?
Motivated teenagers?

"Please help me motivate myself!" Emma asks her high-school teacher in desperation.

"Mum, I'm so bored. I just don't feel like doing anything," Emma complains as she lies apathetically on the sofa after getting home from school, flicking absent-mindedly through the channels on TV, while texting with her left hand on her smartphone.

Parents, teachers and professors are spending more and more time trying to answer the million-dollar question: what can we do to motivate our children, our students? At home we acquire the latest arsenal of equipment to keep them entertained: game consoles, computers, tablets, smartphones, television sets in their bedrooms, DVD players in the car . . . In schools and universities any means may be used to keep students from "getting bored": PowerPoint, Prezi, "flipped classroom", smart boards, tablets . . . Perhaps it will not be long before high schools and universities require that teachers and professors be skilled in singing or dancing in order to "liven up" their classes. As Neil Postman says:

> Teachers, from primary grades through college, are increasing the visual stimulation of their lessons; are reducing the amount of exposition their students must cope with; are relying less on reading and writing assignments; and are reluctantly concluding that the principal means by which student interest may be engaged is entertainment.[1]

This is the age of entertainment, so much so that it seems at times that educators and parents are more engaged in show business than education.

Why is this? We can see at a glance that our children's attention spans are becoming ever shorter. As evidence of this, we need look no further than the increasingly common diagnosis of attention deficit hyperactivity disorder (ADHD), which is one of the main reasons for psychological consultations today. Despite the fact that the causes of ADHD, as well as its treatment, have been the subject of much debate since the 1970s, diagnoses of ADHD in the United States have increased tenfold in the last 20 years. The fact that the US Department of Health and Human Services claims that genetics account only for part of the disorder strongly suggests that non-genetic factors could play an important role in its development.[2] A recent study shows a statistically significant association between higher frequency of digital media use and subsequent symptoms of ADHD.[3] In fact, the prestigious Mayo Clinic recommends limiting screen time for the first five years of life as one of the prevention measures for ADHD.[4] Science has yet to provide an exhaustive, convincing explanation of the origins of ADHD, and so the debate continues.

Furthermore, grandparents claim that today's children "are not like they were in the old days". I do not know what children were like in their day but I do remember that children of my generation did not get out of control in the way that so many appear to do today. We were able to sit in front of a chocolate bar until we were given permission to eat, we knew how to be quiet in shops and waiting rooms, we listened to our parents (at least when they looked serious about it), we spent time playing games in silence, we entertained ourselves with simple, commonplace objects, we did not spend entire days seeking out new sensations, and I cannot recall a single child in my class being medicated for hyperactivity, attention deficit, or anxiety disorders.

"I'm bored!" screams Alex in the paediatrician's waiting room, throwing magazines on the floor as he jumps from seat to seat. His mother runs to the reception desk to ask them to change the channel of the television in the waiting room. One can already see that, at five years old, *Mister Rogers' Neighborhood* or *The Friendly Giant* no longer hold Alex's attention. They finally change the channel to a very fast-paced Japanese animation of gloomy characters fighting each other. "It's fine," his mother thinks to herself, "they're just cartoons." Alex calms down, hypnotised by the screen.

Emma's desperate "Please help me motivate myself!" and Alex's frantic "I'm bored!" resound in the ears of all parents and educators like a cry from nature, protesting because it lacks something that is fundamental for the good of its development. And nature does not forgive ... But what have we done to these children that opposes their nature? In order to answer this question we must ask ourselves the following: What is a child's nature? How do children learn? What drives them to act and learn?

"All grown-ups were once children. (But few of them remember it.)," says Antoine de Saint-Exupéry. Let us try to remember. To rewind for a moment. To rewind the life of Emma, the student who politely but desperately asks her teacher to motivate her. Let us rewind the life of Alex, a child who gets bored with silence or the slow pace of *Mister Rogers*. This seventeen-year-old student and this five-year-old child. Once upon a time, they were both six-month-old babies, small children of one or two years of age. Did Emma ask her mother to "please" motivate her to learn to talk, to crawl toward sockets in the walls, to stand up and pull on the tablecloth, to play, to take her first steps? Did Alex need something more than the sound of the wind in the grass or the discovery of his own shadow to awaken in him a sense of wonder, or a simple story told by his mother to put him to sleep?

Small children do not need us to motivate them *a priori*. Think about it. On Christmas morning, what do our children play with most when they are between six and twenty-four months old? They crawl around, pulling at the ties on the packaging, and they excitedly play with the wrapping paper. The toy is left forgotten. They run behind the balloon we have tied to the handlebars of the bicycle from Santa Claus, shouting, "Santa drank the milk and ate the cookies!" They wonder at the slow fall of the balloon toward the floor.

In the morning, when we are rushing to get them to school on time, they fixate on a shiny, insignificant object on the way:

"Mummy! Wait! Look at that!"
"Hurry up, there's no time!" we reply.

If we are attentive, we can see that small children have a truly remarkable sense of wonder at the small things in life, ordinary details that make up the everyday. Children are especially good at seeing the extraordinary in the ordinary. In fact, it is a privilege reserved to the humble, to those who listen and observe the spectacle of life. The noise made by crinkling wrapping paper, the bubbles in the bath that stick to their little fingers, the tickling sensation caused by an ant walking across their palm, the shimmer of an object found in a puddle. This sense of wonder is what spurs children to discover the world. This is their internal motivation. The smallest things trigger wonder and motivate children to satisfy their curiosity, to learn by themselves how the things around them work, using their own experience with daily life. All this they do of their own volition. At that age, all we have to do is accompany children, preparing an environment for them that is conducive to discovery.

When we provide small children with external stimuli in such a way that these supplant their natural sense of wonder, we override their capacity to motivate themselves. Providing a substitute for what drives children overrides their volition. Ultimately, such children come to depend on external stimuli and are incapable of feeling excitement or wonder about anything. Their irresistible desire to learn is stifled. In some cases, their addiction to overstimulation can cause children to seek out stronger and stronger sensations, which they will then in turn get used to. This will eventually lead them to a state of sustained apathy, lack of enthusiasm, and boredom.

But how can we get young children to undertake things with enthusiasm, to sit quietly while calmly observing their surroundings, to think before acting, to take an interest in the things around them, to be motivated to learn, and to continue to do so as teenagers?

Perhaps the key can be found in two sentences, one written

over seven centuries ago by Thomas Aquinas: "Wonder is the desire to know,"[5] and the other written thousands of years previously by Aristotle: "All men by nature desire to know." Eureka! All we need to do at that early age is protect wonder and allow it to do its work! If "all men by nature desire to know", we can understand how Emma, at only six months of age – without anyone *motivating* her or pushing her from the outside – can have the inner strength and persistence necessary to stretch for the toy that is just out of reach: because it amazes her. If "all men by nature desire to know", we can understand how Emma, at two years of age, can find the internal motivation to pronounce new words. We understand why Alex is content with spending time concentrating on a snail crawling up a window, with discovering the relationship that exists between the movement of his body and the shadow he projects as he walks with his back to the sun. All of these phenomena astonish and amaze children: they trigger wonder, this desire to know. Let us leave the intricacies of learning mechanisms to neuroscientists, developmental linguists and psychologists. This subject is not very relevant here because we are not concerned with the mechanism, but with its origin – and the desire to know, as such, lies beyond the scope of neuroscience.

We want to know what moves Emma to learn, we want to understand where her motivation comes from and under what conditions it operates.

A sense of wonder is what awakens interest in a person. According to a study published in the *Journal of Marketing Research*,[6] a story goes viral on the internet when it provokes awe in its readers. In the study, carried out by the University of Pennsylvania, a series of variables were analysed regarding the spread and communication of various articles from the *New York Times* over a six-month period. Contrary to the popular belief that people look for short content and superficial, frivolous, salacious or morbid stories, the most successful articles were often longer articles with positive content that provoked awe in the readers. The study defines awe as "a feeling of personal transcendence, a sentiment of admiration and elation in the face of something that overwhelms the reader. It causes the spirit to open up and expand, and causes the reader to stop and think."

This is an important discovery for both the world of online marketing and authors of fiction, but it could also be significant from the point of view of learning. Awe, or wonder, is what awakens interest. What if wonder is not merely a feeling? What if wonder is, as Plato and Aristotle claim,[7] the beginning of philosophy? What if we desire to know by nature, as Aristotle suggested? What if wonder pre-exists as something innate in all of us? If this is so, then this discovery has implications that extend far beyond the scope of online marketing. It could be that we have discovered something within the child – wonder – that too often works blindly because it lacks high-quality, beautiful input that can open up the horizons of the mind.

It is well documented that children's neurological make-up – the physical structure of their brain, their "hard drive", so to speak – plays a key role in their development. But is this neurological make-up what drives a child to learn and to act? Those who defend this purely materialistic view of the human being also defend a mechanistic approach to education. According to this point of view, a child is a sort of raw material that can be worked on in order to convert it into what one wants it to be.

According to the mechanistic approach to education, there is no human nature; there is no internal mental state; everything is programmable. Mechanistic educators bombard their children with external stimuli in order to design their neural circuits, with the aim of producing an à la carte child. They also focus on "training in habits" (as mere mechanical repetition of actions), as reflected in John Watson's promise:

> Give me a dozen healthy infants, well-formed, and my own specified world to bring them up in and I'll guarantee to take any one at random and train him to become any type of specialist I might select . . .[8]

This behaviourist view of education sees children as exclusively dependent on their environment for learning. It views the mind as a "black box" that is fully "understood" once the input and the output are observed, defined and, ultimately, perfectly controlled.

However, throughout the history of education, there has always been a keen interest in focusing on internal mental states: on what deeply, intrinsically *motivates* children to learn. Many educators do not feel comfortable with the mechanistic or the behavioural views of education and would agree that the origin of what drives children to learn and to act lies deeper than their neurological make-up, or than a mere black box. T. H. Huxley once remarked:

> How it is that anything so remarkable as a state of conscious-
> ness comes about as the result of irritating nervous tissue,
> is just as unaccountable as the appearance of the Djin when
> Aladdin rubbed his lamp.[9]

More and more people are coming around to the view that the origin of the process is something intangible, immaterial. The Ancient Greeks believed that philosophy originated in wonder, the first manifestation of that intangible quality that moves human beings: the desire to know. Thousands of years later, one of the most renowned pedagogues of our time, Maria Montessori, emphasised the importance of the *interest* in a child's learning process, describing it in many different ways: impulse of "spiritual hunger", polarised attention, internal force. Over the past couple of decades, neuroscience has confirmed many of Montessori's premises, and the education world increasingly tends to call many paradigms of mechanistic learning into question.

So then, if once upon a time there was an Emma and an Alex who desired to know by nature, what happened? How did they lose their sense of wonder? What happened when this wonder disappeared? What can we do to help Emma and Alex wonder again?

Part I

What is wonder?

1

"Why doesn't the rain go up?"

*A child asks, with a perfectly natural curiosity, why the
sunlight comes in through the window, but not through
the wall of the house, and we find it hard to answer him,
because when it comes right down to the heart of the matter
we don't know why. And, moreover, we are so used to our
ignorance in this and a thousand other subjects that there
is something disconcerting, almost shocking, in having our
mental apathy stirred by a call to action.*

Dorothy Canfield Fisher

*The fascination of children lies in this: that with each of
them all things are remade, and the universe is put again
upon its trial.*

G. K. Chesterton

We have seen that wonder is what deeply motivates a child, but why
does reality inspire such a response in children? What is it that causes
them to wonder at their surroundings? Let us attempt to get to the
bottom of the mechanism of wonder using some illustrations.

In the 2010 movie *Alice in Wonderland*, just before she finds the
courage to do the impossible – slay the dragon – Alice says to the
Mad Hatter, "Sometimes I believe in as many as six impossible things
before breakfast." Wonderland is the land of the impossible: a talking
cat, a cake that makes you grow, a rabbit obsessed with the time . . .
an infinite display of impossibilities. In other words, a country seen
through the eyes of a child.

A child's capacity to think of impossible things is marvellous. "Mummy, why doesn't the rain go up?" "Why don't bees make jam or syrup?" "Why aren't ants lazy?"

These questions often annoy us, for various reasons. We have no time to waste with these silly thoughts. They are not useful questions. Who cares why ants aren't lazy? We worry because our child is wasting time instead of doing something more important, like learning Mandarin or developing an interest in computer programming. What is more, it seems like the child is seeking an explanation for something that cannot be explained, or, even worse, that they want to change the established order of things. It can even become a cause for worry: Is my child normal? How can he come up with such ideas? Who put that into her head? Maybe he has too much free time?

When our two-, three- and four-year-old children bombard us with questions that seem illogical, they are not seeking or demanding an explanation. They are not looking to change the established order of things. It is simply their way of admiring a reality that *is*, but that could just as easily *not have been*. As mentioned above, Plato and Aristotle said that wonder is the beginning of philosophy. Thus, when these impossible questions arise in our children's little heads, they are simply philosophising! Children philosophise because they are astonished by *any* reality – including the natural laws of our world – for the simple reason that it *exists*. When a baby is born, it first sees its mother, then it discovers more family members, a passer-by on the street, a flower, an insect, a rock, the moon, a shadow, gravity, light . . . As G. K. Chesterton said:

> As we walk the streets and see below us those delightful bulbous heads, three times too big for the body, which mark these human mushrooms, we ought always primarily to remember that within every one of these heads there is a new universe, as new as it was on the seventh day of creation.[1]

Wonder is the desire to know. Seeing things with new eyes allows us to marvel at their very existence, wanting to know about them again and again, as if it were for the first time. Small children have a sense of wonder because they do not take the world for granted; instead, they see it as a gift. This type of metaphysical thought is unique to people who can see that things *are*, but equally could *never have been*. We are – the world is – contingent: if we cease to exist the world goes on. Nevertheless, we are part of something greater than ourselves, and the natural mechanism of wonder is precisely what allows us to transcend our everyday existence to experience it. As a result, wonder leads us to an attitude of profound humility and gratitude.

Wonder is an innate mechanism in children; they are born with it. As Aristotle puts it, they desire to know *by nature*. But in order for wonder to blossom, children must be given an environment that respects it. And how is this done? It is true that wonder is an intangible reality that cannot be identified or measured by science, but what does science say about the desire to know? Is the learning process exclusively dependent on the environment? And if not, what is its relationship with this environment?

2

Exclusively dependent on the environment for learning?

All mankind is divided into three classes: those that are immovable, those that are movable, and those that move.

Benjamin Franklin

How do children develop? Do they have what it takes within themselves to develop in a normal environment, or do they depend exclusively on the intervention of external stimulation? Does the learning process of children start from within, aided by contact with reality, or is it carried out exclusively from without by means of continual bombardment with external stimuli to which a child is passively subjected?

In the last century, pedagogues, psychologists and neuroscientists have dedicated themselves to answering this question. In the first half of the last century, Montessori caused a revolution in the world of pedagogy when she spoke of the "sensitive periods" of a child in the first years of life, specifying that education consisted in a development whose primary agent is the child. She affirmed that the process is initiated within the child, through an *irresistible force*, while the environment and the teacher are mere facilitators. Although this development occurs through the senses and exposure to the external world, she says that this outer world has no significance as such for the child. She says that it merely "provides the necessary means for psychic life, just as the body, by eating and breathing, takes from its outer environment the necessary means of physical life."[1]

This revolutionary approach has long been a cause of scandal, owing to the way it clashes with the rigidly utilitarian and behaviourist

14

approach that characterises the educational system at times. For some, respect for the spontaneous activity of children in preschool may not "assure the acquisition of knowledge and abilities" according to the milestones that are, by consensus, considered necessary for a child beginning primary school to have reached. When the mechanistic approach is adopted in preschool, the starting point is always milestones. First, some milestones are established according to what society considers useful, or according to what a child does or knows on average, and then methods are put in place to ensure that each child achieves them. In other words, everything is programmable.

Beginning in the 1940s, a series of psychologists[*] marked the course of neuropsychology and developmental psychology with a set of experiments carried out on rats. One of these concluded that rats that were trained as pets achieved better results when it came to problem solving than did rats kept in cages. Another experiment compared a group of rats living in cages with others that were surrounded by toys, tunnels, ladders, wheels, etc., and it was noticed that there was an increase in the size of the cerebral cortex of the rats living in an enriched environment. These experiments, and others later performed, gave rise to the theory of cerebral plasticity, which put an end to the popular belief that the structure of the brain was fixed from the time of birth. The plasticity of the brain confirmed the importance Montessori placed on sensory experiences during the sensitive period between zero and three years of age. However, these experiments also gave rise to the conclusion that optimal learning required an *enriched environment*.

These findings were accompanied by studies carried out in some orphanages, in some of which it was found that a severe lack of stimulation often gave rise to various psychological and learning disorders, such as ADHD and attachment disorders.

In 1965, an early intervention programme called the Head Start programme emerged in the United States as an effort to assist children in the following situations of risk: 1) children with a low socio-economic status, 2) children with developmental disorders, and

---

[*]   Among these were Donald Hebb and Mark Rosenzweig.

3) children at risk as a result of a premature birth. The billions of dollars that were invested in this programme gave rise to numerous studies on the success of early intervention for children in situations of risk. Some concluded that there were no benefits, others asserted that they had detected some improvements, while others did identify improvements, but not for all ages; not always sustained; and not in all areas.[2]

The belief that an enriched environment was key for learning gave rise to the desire to go beyond early intervention programmes for children in situations of risk. As a result, "early learning programmes" for healthy children began to spring up throughout the world, with a general tendency to associate success with reaching various educational milestones through an enriched environment. These programmes further maintain that all aspects of a child must be adequately stimulated in order for him or her to develop appropriately for his or her age. If children do not achieve the milestones previously marked in some area, a corrective action is taken that tends to consist of exercises with the objective of normalising the area in which there was a supposed developmental delay. According to this method, children are entities moved from without through artificial stimuli: the learning process is exclusively dependent on their environment. The main premise appears to be *the more, the better*, so that parents are advised to stimulate their children as much and as soon as possible.

An example of "early learning" programmes for healthy children can be found in Glenn Doman's "Gentle Revolution", through books such as *How to Teach Your Baby to Read*, *How Smart is Your Baby?*, *How to Teach your Baby Math*, and *How to Multiply Your Baby's Intelligence*, among others. To date, there are no studies that support the success of these "accelerated learning" programmes with healthy children.[3] In fact, decades of studies appear to confirm that the key to healthy development resides in the quality of the relationship children have with their principal caregiver during the first years of life. The importance of secure attachment fostered by this relationship cannot be overstated.† Removing normal and healthy children from

---

†   The attachment theory, initially developed by John Bowlby and Mary Ainsworth, has become the theory *par excellence* from which

their principal caregiver during their first years of life with the excuse that they need stimulation in order to achieve better results is a grave error.

In 2007, the English Economic and Social Research Council published a document to which seventeen experts from various European universities contributed, with the intention of increasing dialogue between neuroscience and education. In it, the following was stated: "Contrary to much popular belief, there is no convincing neuroscientific case for starting formal education as early as possible."[4]

The document explains, among other things, that brain plasticity is a phenomenon that lasts throughout life, not only during one's early years. Additionally, the experiments with rats do *not* demonstrate that an enriched environment is necessary for healthy brain development, but only point to a total absence of stimulation being detrimental to learning. In fact, a 2012 study indicates that overstimulation of newborn mice leads to deficits in cognitive performance.[5] The natural environment of rats (or human beings) is much richer than an artificial environment built with cages, ladders and tunnels. The familiar natural environment of children is not one with a total absence of stimuli. On the whole, there is evidence that confirms that the absence of stimuli can harm a child, but, on the other hand, there is no evidence that demonstrates that the enrichment of a normal environment can improve his or her development. Furthermore, as we shall see next, certain evidence has begun to come out that indicates that overstimulation can create other problems for children, such as inattention, impulsivity and loss of interest in learning.

An increasing number of studies[6] now discuss the existence of a series of "neuromyths" in the field of education. The Organisation for Economic Co-operation and Development (OECD) defines the neuromyth as a "misconception generated by a misunderstanding, a

---

investigation in the area of child development finds its focus. Empirical evidence has confirmed the attachment theory in numerous areas, such as psychology, neuroscience, and pedagogy, to the point of its forming the basis of the majority of social and educational policies of numerous countries.

misreading or a misquote of facts scientifically established (by brain research) to make a case for use of brain research in education or other contexts".[7] Two of these myths are related to what has been discussed above:

1. **The first-three-years myth**: the belief that there is a critical period during the first three years of life, an absolute window in time beyond which certain areas of learning cannot be influenced any more.
2. **The enrichment myth**: the belief according to which enriched environments enhance the brain's capacity for learning.

Studies also warn against commercial programmes, such as Brain Gym™, founded on the false belief that neurological mechanisms like reading can be influenced by specific physical exercises such as the "cross-crawl" and "hook-up", which are claimed to balance the cerebral hemispheres. To date, it has never been scientifically established that these or other similar programmes lead to positive results.[8] This is similarly the case with the thousands of DVDs, CDs, apps and devices that capitalise on the first-three-years myth, claiming to improve the intelligence of our children and further encouraging popular belief in such unproven methods.[9]

According to a poll carried out in the United States, 62% of parents believe that educational games and "sound books" (books with an audio component) are very important for the intellectual development of children; 49% say the same of educational DVDs; and 43% believe it of video games.[10] The North American children's entertainment industry has powerful means of convincing parents of the benefits of its products. For example, a study indicates that sales of DVDs for preschoolers alone is no less than 30% of the market share of the industry, and over 80% of the top selling paid apps in the Education category of the iTunes Store target children.[11] Yet various other studies demonstrate that there is no relationship between the consumption of these products and the acquisition of speech or foreign languages before the age of two.[12] Some studies even go as far as establishing a relationship between the early consumption of educational DVDs and a decrease in the vocabulary and cognitive development of babies.[13] As for children between two and five years old, the evidence is mixed, with outcomes seeming to differ depending on the nature of the content.[14]

In 2017, the Canadian Paediatric Society stated that "there are no proven benefits of media exposure for infants and toddlers, and some known developmental risks," and "preschoolers learn best from live, direct and dynamic interactions with caring adults." In short, it recommends that the use of digital media by children less than two years old be avoided altogether, concluding that "there is no evidence to support introducing technology at an early age."[15]

The American Academy of Pediatrics similarly signals that studies have not found evidence that there are clear educational benefits in providing such exposure to children less than eighteen months old, while there are studies that instead warn of the potential danger of screens to the health and development of children in this age group.[16] Both paediatric associations recommend that children from two to five years use digital media for no more than one hour a day, and only with adult supervision. They add that media content must be good quality and slow-paced, and warn against the temptation of using digital media to calm children down, as doing so could impede the development of normal self-control. They recommend that digital media not be used for an hour before sleeping, and never during the night, as well as insisting that bedrooms, mealtimes and playtimes be free of screens. Paediatricians conclude that parents do not have to feel pressured to introduce the use of technology early on, as user interfaces are intuitive, and children will quickly learn to use them when the time comes. This may then naturally prompt the question: what do children truly need for a healthy development in place of technological stimuli?

Dan Siegel, an expert in neurobiology at the University of California in Los Angeles, gives us a hint:

> There is no need to bombard infants or young children (or possibly anyone) with excessive sensory stimulation in hopes of "building better brains." This is an unfortunate

misinterpretation of the neurobiological literature – that somehow "more is better." It just is not so. Parents and other caregivers can "relax" and stop worrying about providing huge amounts of sensory bombardment for their children. This synaptic overproduction during the early years of life has been proposed to allow for a likelihood that the brain will develop properly within the "average" environment that will supply the necessary minimal amount of sensory stimulation [. . .].

He adds:

More important than excessive sensory stimulation in the early years of development, however, are the patterns of interaction between child and caregiver. Attachment research suggests that collaborative interpersonal interaction, not excessive sensory stimulation, can be seen as the key to healthy development.[17] *[Emphasis added]*

We notice, then, that the process begins within the child and is carried out through sensory experiences of the reality that surrounds him or her, mainly through human relationships, as Siegel affirms. Siegel suggests that there might be something *within us* that enables or gives life to cerebral development; that behind the developmental process that forms the brain, there is a non-material principle, the "psyche" or the "mind" – as real as a lung or heart – that acts, but that cannot be seen even with modern technological devices. Some call this intangible reality human soul, others the intellect; it is no coincidence that the spiritual leaders of the world are interested in Siegel's approach. In 1999, Pope John Paul II invited Dan Siegel to give a conference in the Vatican called "Toward a Biology of Compassion"[18] and in 2009, Siegel took part in a panel at a conference called "The Scientific Basis for Compassion" with the Dalai Lama.

Whatever our beliefs may be, the vast majority of parents, scientists and educators share the point of view that a human being is driven by something intangible. Plato said that the beginning of philosophy was wonder, the first manifestation of something outside the realm of the purely physical that moves a human being: "the desire to know", as Thomas Aquinas described it. Chesterton spoke of wonder as something that drives a person, not the consequence of external stimuli: "This elementary wonder, however, is not a mere fancy derived from the fairy tales; on the contrary, all the fire of the fairy tales is derived from this."[19]

Perhaps the intangible "something" referred to by Siegel that cannot be measured with modern technological instruments confirms what Plato, Aquinas and Chesterton wrote. Perhaps one's neurological make-up does not, in itself, explain everything. If this is the case, and we think that it is, we can come to an understanding of how revolutionary this discovery is; realise to what degree wonder plays a key role in the development of a child; and consider how much harm can be done by losing it in early childhood. If it is true that a child does not need more than a "minimal amount of sensory stimulation . . . within the 'average' environment," as stated by Siegel, then we can ask ourselves what happens to children who are subjected to an excessively enriched environment in which they are consistently overstimulated from without.

3

Consequences of overstimulation

What information consumes is rather obvious: it consumes the attention of its recipients. Hence a wealth of information creates a poverty of attention . . .

Herbert Simon, Nobel Prize recipient
(the quote is from 1971, before the introduction of the internet)

If children's inclination for learning begins from within, what are the consequences of acting as if the process has its origin exclusively in the environment, in stimulating children as much as possible? What happens if we give them a sustained stimulation that they do not need?

Not only has it been demonstrated that an external bombardment of stimuli does not make young children smarter, but, in the last decade, studies have begun to come out that relate overstimulation with learning difficulties. In 2011, Dimitri Christakis, director of the Center for Child Health, Behavior and Development at Seattle Children's Research Institute, and one of the world experts on the relationship between television content and child development, published a study in the journal *Pediatrics* that relates watching *SpongeBob SquarePants* and difficulties with learning and self-control.[1]

A class of four-year-old children was divided into three groups. The first group was exposed to nine minutes of the fast-paced show *SpongeBob SquarePants*, the second to nine minutes of the slow-paced show *Caillou*, and the third was instructed to draw a picture.

The children were all given a number of small tests afterward, and those exposed to *SpongeBob* scored twelve points lower than the rest of the children. Later, the children exposed to *SpongeBob* were able to wait only two and a half minutes before eating a snack, while those who were exposed to *Caillou* and those who had drawn a picture were able to wait quietly for four minutes. The study had its limitations, due to the small sample size and because there was no investigation over an extended period of time into whether the consequences would last. However, what we do know is that over-stimulation is present in a sustained manner in the environment in which the vast majority of children find themselves today and the con-sequences we observe around us seem to confirm, rather than refute, these findings.

Christakis believes that the problem is that *SpongeBob* is extremely fast-paced for small children. The same goes, therefore, for films like *Cars*, *The Incredibles*, *Ice Age* and *Minions,* as well as others that are supposedly for infants or small children, but are not suited for these ages, or are made for older children or teenagers but are in reality often watched by children under the age of five. Such movies and television series are often designed to entertain parents, not to contribute to the healthy development of children. In fact, in another North American study,[2] 59 supposedly educational DVDs directed at children under three were analysed. An average of seven and a half abrupt scene changes per minute was identified, which is ordinarily impossible for children to experience in their day-to-day lives. It should not surprise us that children get bored, impatient and nervous when we turn the pace of the real world on its head! The study on *SpongeBob* is in line with various others that associate con-sumption of television and video games with attentional problems[3] and watching violent shows before the age of three with attentional problems and impulsiveness by the age of seven.[4] Prestigious North American paediatricians went as far as issuing the message *primum no nocere* ("first, do no harm"), a maxim attributed to Hippocrates and applied in the field of medicine, in order to raise awareness in the scientific community of the importance of discouraging screen use during early childhood.[5]

As Siegel said, children need an "average" environment, a minimal amount of sensory stimulation . . . No more, no less. We do not have to draw neural circuits with chalk in our children's little brains. There is an internal motor that drives children to want to discover things on their own: wonder. The primary agent in education is not the methodology that is used, nor the amount of stimuli that are targeted at the child, nor yet the educator. Children themselves are the primary agents of their education. The principal caregiver acts as an intermediary between a child and reality, as a base for exploration. If the attachment with the caregiver is secure (in other words, if the child trusts that his or her principal caregiver's attention is unconditional), the child feels safe and will continually go further to explore. If there is not a secure attachment between the child and his principal caregiver, the child will be insecure and will not explore his or her surroundings with confidence. Parents who think that, after a day of work, they must be entertainers for their children can rest easy. Quality is not measured by the quantity of stimuli that a child receives. Simply being present and establishing a bond with them, feeding them, looking at them, speaking softly to them, smiling at them, caressing them, is enough. Six-month-old infants are content with examining their hands; they do not need talking dolls, revolving mobiles above their crib, or music to put them to sleep every night. Nine-month-olds are happy to pull out grass and put it in their mouths. Twelve-month-olds are thrilled by their father playing peek-a-boo with them from behind the door of their bedroom and with stretching out their arm to reach the shelf of canned tomatoes. As Chesterton said:

> When we are very young children we do not need fairy tales:
> we only need tales. Mere life is interesting enough. A child
> of seven is excited by being told that Tommy opened a door
> and saw a dragon. But a child of three is excited by being told
> that Tommy opened a door.[6]

For a small child, overstimulation can be found in details that an adult who is not very sensitive, or who has difficulty seeing things from the child's perspective, barely perceives. For example,

Christakis tells us that a television show with intermittent flashes of light, scene changes, fast movements, sharp transitions, etc. can be overstimulating for the developing brains of small children, and can potentially have adverse effects on them.[7] There are studies that relate time spent watching television in childhood with a greater risk of attentional and learning disorders, with a decrease in the interest of the student in the classroom and in grades in mathematics, and with a lesser likelihood of attending post-secondary education.[8] Bright and flashy screens displaying loud and fast-paced content disturb the only true and sustainable learning that exists in a child: that of discovering and rediscovering the world for oneself and at one's own pace, with a sense of wonder that goes beyond mere curiosity for the unknown or interest in novelty.

Now, let us leave the studies aside and turn to common sense alone. What happens when a child is overstimulated? Children who are not used to overstimulation will have a protective response when faced with a saturation of the senses. In a newborn, this reaction is seen when the baby closes its eyes, jerking its head from left to right and back again, in an attempt to escape from what it perceives as an aggression. In a two-, three- or four-year-old who is not used to it, overstimulation can induce fear, tears, or interior tension. This is what happens when, for example, a small child goes to see a movie for the first time. What happens if children are continuously under the effect of overstimulation; when they immediately get all they want and so have not learned to wait or to experience frustration; when their agendas are as full (of extracurricular activities) as that of a stressed-out CEO; when they are not sleeping the minimum number of hours required for their age; when they are bombarded by methodologies that aim at accelerating their development; when they are surrounded by screens with loud noises and fast-paced content; or when they are asked to carry out multiple activities at one time? Human beings have a great capacity for adapting to their environment, but our nature has limitations. And when one challenges nature's limitations, nature does not forgive and may produce all kinds of undesirable collateral effects. Among other things, children can become preconditioned to expect high levels of stimulation, eventually leading to inattention.

The saturation of the senses that results from this provokes the following vicious circle:

1. Overstimulation replaces children's natural drive and overrides and deadens their sense of wonder.
2. After a fleeting sensation of euphoria, they settle down, become passive, stop taking initiative, get bored, and allow mental laziness to overcome them. They display apathy, but an agitated apathy, because they are accustomed – or, to put it better, addicted – to the overstimulation and want more. Overstimulation predisposes them to want to live in a higher and higher stimulus environment.
3. They become hyperactive and nervous, do not like being still, and like to attract the attention of adults by breaking the rules. They need to seek new, continually more intense, entertainment or sensations in order to alleviate their addiction to overstimulation. When they encounter it, they calm down, like an anxious smoker who lights up a cigarette. This is the reason children calm down when we turn on screens in the car or in the waiting room, or why an overstimulated newborn only falls asleep during a car ride.
4. The background noise of overstimulation that they are used to increases and the vicious circle continues to turn with renewed vigour. The telecommunications industry and the media respond in proportion to the stimulation they need, with increasingly aggressive, shocking and fast-paced content. Some of the television series that we parents used to watch are digitally remade for them with faster-paced content. They see explicit violence in the news and in video games, and the stories in movies or literature to which they are exposed are filled with blood, sex, monsters, vampires or romance stories that they are not mature enough to understand.

5. These overstimulated children then become precocious children or teenagers who have "seen and done it all". They are saturated, and their irresistible desire to learn is stifled. Some of these teenagers, like Emma, will ask their parents and teachers if they can help them motivate themselves. Others will seek "entertainment" through other types of activities: vandalism, sexting, (cyber)bullying, binge drinking, drugs, etc., using the people they involve in these activities as a means of "having fun".

"Kids today are not like they were in the old days," grandparents remark. It is true. Nowadays, it is necessary to look for wonder in children of earlier and earlier ages in order to find it. We note that children, and then teenagers, are increasingly distracted and hyperactive; have difficulty forming bonds, recognising authority, and managing their emotions; have attitudes at times violent and unappreciative; and find their source of motivation mainly from external artificial stimulation.

Once, a five-year-old child could marvel at *Mister Rogers' Neighborhood*. Now, a child would find it boring. And the same goes for *Caillou*, *Postman Pat* and *Dora the Explorer*. Once, a person would have watched *E.T.* at the age of six, *The Goonies* at twelve, and *Poltergeist* as an adult. Now, many five-year-olds would hardly bat an eyelid before the terror and suspense of *Poltergeist*, would get bored with *The Goonies*, and would not for a minute put up with the slow pace of *E.T.* Instead, they are used to seeing their older brother playing *Call of Duty* or *Grand Theft Auto*. The nature of children has not changed; children are children and will always be so. It is the environment in which they find themselves that has changed, that submits them to stimuli that impede them from enjoying a slower-paced film. They look up the current weather conditions on a smartphone before they so much as take a look through the window. In fact, they live in a world with more screens than windows. Before, children's immediate environments would tend to be real and adapted to their pace and their needs. Now, it is they who must adapt to the frenzied pace of an environment that produces increasingly more stimuli. Television, smartphones, social networks, chats, gaming consoles, never-ending extracurricular activities, fewer hours of sleep, earlier school enrolment, talking toys, etc. As Montessori noted:

> When it is observed that the child reacts by withdrawing into himself, turning away from his parents, displaying inertia, discouragement, capriciousness and other unexpected behavior, the adults in charge seldom draw the conclusion that they are in the presence of a cry or a protest from nature – whether it is a cry to the educators to discover if they have not imposed on the child something very repugnant to him, or whether they have deprived him of something which is indispensable to his development.[9]

When educators see this protest from a child, they can, without knowing it, respond in such a way that the child enters into a vicious circle that worsens the situation. Or they intensify their discipline and again stubbornly deny the child his or her basic needs; or do not respect the child's pace and rhythms, including that of sleep; or they fill the child's schedule with extracurricular activities; or they throw in the towel and give in to the child's every whim, increasingly saturating his or her senses; or putting on a DVD to relieve the child's addiction; or giving him or her a tablet or a fidget spinner, for example. In fact, there is no shortage of toys that have claimed to calm hyperactive children, like the infamous fidget spinner, which was a failed attempt to help distracted children to focus their attention. But as can be expected, there is no evidence[10] that confirms the benefits of the fidget spinner, since it is only a "quick fix", or periodic relief for children who are addicted to a fast pace. We must not confuse wonder with passive fascination. Wonder is active; it is expectant and open in the face of reality. Fascination, on the other hand is passive; it is dependent on external stimuli.

The fact is that there is no magic formula for children to recover their capacity for sustained attention; this is only achieved through a return to a slower pace that harmonises with their interior order. It should therefore surprise no one that fidget spinners are currently banned in many classrooms. In each of these cases, such devices or toys only serve to aggravate the downward spiral and make it increasingly difficult to resolve the problem at its roots.

The intensity of the downward spiral varies from one child to another, depending on the quantity of stimuli and on the duration of the situation of overstimulation throughout the day and through the years. In any case, it makes sense that a child placed in this situation will ask for more entertainment, like Alex, and will end up with a stifled desire to learn that Emma and her teachers would call "lack of motivation".

Blaise Pascal said that, "All of man's problems stem from his inability to sit quietly in a room alone." Children who have not initiated the downward spiral of overstimulation will be intellectually curious, independently of their intellectual potential, if in addition to not giving them ready-made answers, we have let them discover at their own pace through spontaneous activity. They will be curious, discoverers, inventors, capable of questioning without being bothered by uncertainty, of formulating hypotheses and of verifying their validity by means of observation. They will calmly observe plants, flowers, snails and butterflies. They will put a piece of paper next to the pincers of an earwig to see what the insect does with it. They will play with their shadow, wondering why the image reflected in the mirror always mimics them, or how Mary Poppins went up the chimney, defying the laws of gravity. On the beach or in their own backyard, they will begin to invent treasures to dig up; in the forest they will imagine cabins that could be built from a tree. All these questions and adventures that stem from the wonder of our little philosophers, if they find the necessary fertile environment, are the preamble to a still deeper reflection on the mysteries and laws of our world.

When these children filled with wonder reach adolescence, it will be more natural for them to study because their learning will be preceded by a genuine desire to learn, not by external motivations. What will drive them to study will be their desire to know, not their desire to merely win approval or improve their school results. It is true that the teenager of every era has certain traits that wonder will not cure – precisely because adolescence is not a disease, but rather another developmental stage with its own proper characteristics. However, for teenagers whose desire to know has been respected in childhood, it will be more natural to read novels and find enjoyment in the long and beautiful descriptions of places and characters. They will not be bored by the writings of authors like Charles Dickens, J. R. R. Tolkien or C. S. Lewis.

4

The mechanistic approach

In the past the man has been first; in the future the system must be first . . . the first object of any good system must be that of developing first-class men.

Frederick W. Taylor, father of the mechanistic theory
in organised labour

The mere idea that something cruel can be useful is in itself immoral.

Cicero

The mechanistic approach to early education consists of marking milestones in childhood, and applying external methods, or "accelerated learning tips", to ensure each child can achieve these milestones. This approach, disconnected from the reality of the needs and possibilities of each child, considers them as programmable entities, standardised products; in short, as a means to an end. In this educational approach, milestones are marked according to the average, which is to say, according to the expectations for children of a certain age, which are prescribed by the curve based on the average of what children of a given age do or know. When children depart from the curve because they have not started crawling at a certain age, because they don't know to identify the colours at the age of two, because they cannot write their name or know their numbers up to 100 at the age of four, then the alarm is sounded and measures are taken to remedy the situation. There are more and more children medicated to facilitate learning at earlier and earlier ages. There are more and more children falling asleep in classrooms because their extracurricular activities do not fit into their schedules. There are more and more children needing psychological support or repeating courses. A preschool once suggested that a mother make her five-year-old daughter repeat a year because she found reading and writing difficult. How can it be that we have reached such extremes if, before the first-three-years myth flooded our classrooms, children had always begun to read and write after the age of six or seven?

The creation of milestones to ensure that children remain *normal* – because they follow the curve – is only one step away from the race to create a *superchild*. And so every child who is not such a *superchild* is potentially considered *abnormal*, which is largely where we find ourselves today. There are more and more parents who fill the heads and schedules of their children with extracurricular and school activities in order to accelerate their child's development, with the logical consequence of the curve – and the mean of the curve – shifting. If it was once acceptable to learn to read, write and count at the age of six or seven, some now advocate beginning at two or three.

In that sense, the obsession with utility and productivity in education often detracts from the importance of other dimensions of education – such as the arts, for example, because they are considered useless.

> "What good does it do you, Socrates, to learn the lyre if you are going to die?"
>
> "To play the lyre before I die."

The criterion of utility can be a trap that blinds us to what is truly valuable.

All in all, the mechanistic methods have triumphed for years because they are useful – and nothing that is useful is typically questioned . . . until it stops being so, of course. But now we are at a turning point, because we are witnessing disenchantment with this approach to education. We have realised that using external rewards and punishments to achieve short-term objectives has little, if anything, to do with education.

5

Educating versus inculcating

*The task of the modern educator is not to cut down jungles,
but to irrigate deserts.*

C. S. Lewis

Faced with situations like the lack of self-control in children like Alex
and the lack of motivation in students like Emma, some pedagogues
speak of the need to return to the practice of *inculcating* in children
good habits and the value of a good work ethic. We have hit upon one
of the symptoms, but to apply the appropriate remedy, we must make
a diagnosis based on the main cause that gave rise to this string of
problems. Children are apathetic, unappreciative; they expect us to
entertain them, to *motivate* them, because we have spoon-fed them
everything; we have replaced their natural process of discovery of
the world – their sense of wonder. Clearly, *inculcating* does not seem
an appropriate means of recovering wonder, because it implies an
external action on the subject rather than an attempt to re-awaken that
which is innate.

If we look at the etymological roots of *inculcate*, we find the
following: *inculcare*; from *in-* meaning "towards the interior", and
calcis meaning "heel". Originally, it had the sense of using the heel to
forcefully hammer something into something else. Hence its current
meaning of forcefully instilling an idea or concept into another without inviting that person to understand and accept it – or to reinforce
it, persistently teaching or stubbornly imposing one's own arbitrary
opinion.

Inculcating implies an external and foreign action on a passive
subject. It is a mechanistic technique that does not achieve sustainable

results because its subjects do not make what is presented to them their own. Inculcating erases the child, replacing him or her with an external imprint.

On the other hand, the etymological root of *educate* is completely the opposite. *Ex* and *ducere*: to accompany, drawing the best out of someone from the inside out. This approach relies on the child because it assumes that the desire to know comes from within, not from without.

What is the difference between the points of view of the educator and the inculcator? The paradigm of the educator is that of *receiving*, while that of the inculcator is that of *imposing*. The educator accepts children as they are and accompanies them in reaching the perfection of which their nature is capable, surrounding them with opportunities so that they can achieve this on their own, and protecting their gaze from what is not suitable for them. To accept children as they are means to avoid projecting the intricacies and complexities of the adult world on them. Sometimes we tend to attribute to them all sorts of petty intentions that they are not old enough to experience or even to understand. Small children are innocent, incapable of malicious thoughts or twisted intentions.

Accepting others as they are makes us all more human. To accept children as they are is to recognise that they are the protagonists of their own life stories, that they have certain basic needs, certain rhythms that are not our own.

On the other hand, the *inculcator* acts according to his or her own interests, not those of the child, trying to bring the child in line with them. If we cannot accept others as they are before we start giving something to them, our gift is an imposition because it is self-interested. It is an imposition that puts strain on them. "I will give you this, but in exchange you must produce and adopt a series of behaviours that I like." How many times have we heard people say (perhaps it has escaped us also), "I'm doing it for your own good"? And the response of the child, if he or she could realise what was happening and speak, would no doubt be: "Which do you love more, me or what you call 'my own good'? First, love me, accept me as I am. Then, you will naturally love what is good for me, guiding me, giving me opportunities to be better, surrounding me with what suits my nature, and protecting me from what does not." How easy it is to confuse ends with means! The end of education is the child, not what we claim to achieve with him or her.

Instilling our ideas into someone else is not the way to go about educating. Inculcated citizens tend to be dependent on penalties and impositions found in laws and ethical codes because they have not learned to act appropriately of their own accord, but instead have always been told how to do so. They live by *incentives*, because they are used to rewards that condition all of their non-free behaviours.

We are on a crusade for freedom, but there have never been so many people who are "remote-controlled" in their life by the latest fashions. There is no freedom without volition – and authentic voli- tion is motivation from within. It is quite significant that there has never been as much business and self-help literature on the theme of motivation as there is now. When wonder is deadened, one lives one's whole life searching for external substitutes. On a business level, companies hire consultants to carry out surveys to understand why employees are or are not motivated. They hire coaches to implement motivational techniques to increase profits. As parents, we look for easy formulas for getting children to sleep, eat, obey, and "behave themselves". On a personal level, we read self-help books, placing our faith in them and all sorts of philosophies of life in an attempt to boost our willpower. Instead of living from the inside out, we live from the outside in. We lean toward simple formulas: the title of nearly every self-help book starts with "10 Steps to . . ." We often do not have the time to delve deeper.

We must go to the heart of the matter. What we need to change, in order for the culture of the bare minimum to change, is not children, nor teenagers, but the approach that we have in regards to their edu- cation. We need to stop *inculcating* and start *drawing out the best in them*. Einstein said that, "We can't solve problems by using the same kind of thinking we used when we created them." If children do not exert themselves because the loss of wonder has erased and stifled their irresistible desire to know, we must help them to rediscover it. We must create home and preschool environments that are conducive to wonder. How is this done? By respecting children's sensitivity, their spontaneous movement, their innate curiosity that drives them to discover, their natural pace and rhythms, their phases of childhood; encouraging unstructured play, rituals, mystery and silence; and surrounding them with beauty.

In the next section of this book, we will delve deeper into each one of these ideas.

Part II

What is the Wonder Approach?

6

Guided discovery learning

*We spend the first year of a child's life teaching it to walk
and talk and the rest of its life to shut up and sit down.
There's something wrong there.*

Neil deGrasse Tyson

*If discipline is founded upon liberty, the discipline itself
must necessarily be active. We do not consider an individual
disciplined only when he has been rendered as artificially
silent as a mute and as immovable as a paralytic. He is an
individual annihilated, not disciplined.*

Maria Montessori, *The Montessori Method*

Wonder is the desire to know. But is there no need for learning to have
at least minimal structure? What good can come from discovery in
chaos? What about discipline?

Spontaneous inventiveness or discovery on one hand, and discipline or guidance on the other, seem to be contradictory concepts, but
that is not the case. Pablo Picasso said: "Inspiration exists, but it must
find you at work." And Einstein, who was never lacking in humour,
proposed the following formula for success:

A (success) = X (work) + Y (play) + Z (keeping your mouth shut)

If one does not carry out one's work in the state of interior freedom that characterises a playful attitude, one will always depend on
external stimuli – rewards and punishments – and so it will be difficult
to achieve anything that is truly meaningful for oneself. Here, "play"

does not refer to the sort of *passive entertainment* experienced by someone who goes to the movie theatre or turns on the television "to see if I'll come across something that's any good," or by that child who, stretched out on the sofa, turns to the PlayStation as the first and final recourse to stave off boredom. *Play* can be understood in the sense of enjoying a task because one does it with heart, imagination and creativity; one internalises it and makes it one's own. This type of play is perfectly compatible with effort, because it is an active, not passive, play. Like that child who spends hours in silence, concentrating, making a castle from sand, water and little pebbles on the seashore, or the child who builds a fort by draping sheets over the dining room furniture.

The same philosopher who related wonder with learning, Thomas Aquinas, also wrote about the two ways of acquiring knowledge: 1) through *invention or discovery* and 2) through *discipline and learning*,[1] where another person guides the learner's reasoning.

According to him, discovery is the "more perfect" way.[2] In fact, learning, whether it be through instruction or not, always involves discovery – the learner's participation and engagement in what is taught – because all learning involves a synthesis of previously acquired knowledge and new material. As Thomas Aquinas says, "all teaching proceeds from pre-existing knowledge."[3] Therefore, children must, on their own, begin to fit new learning into the structure of what they already know. No one can perform this work of *discovery* or *assimilation* for them, however good a teacher he or she might be. Teachers can guide them through this process, but are no substitute for the child's own natural desire to know.

Montessori and modern neuroscience suggest that we are not exclusively dependent on experience, but rather, *we are expectant of it*. Children possess a natural inclination to proactively search for meaning and knowledge that consists, among other things, in fitting something new into what they already know. Not only do we underestimate this quality, but we are ignorant of it and erase it with a continual bombardment of external stimuli.

Discovery and discipline are not opposite, but rather complementary, concepts. On one hand, one must accompany children, who are agents of their own learning, and create favourable conditions for their spontaneous discovery. It is not necessary to motivate children *a priori*, presenting them with extraordinary and spectacular things in order to move them to act in a predetermined manner. On the other hand, we must structure the transmission of knowledge through our guidance, relying on children's pre-existing knowledge and motivation. In early childhood, structure should be minimal and must serve to facilitate invention and discovery, through spontaneous movement or play. This can be done through a careful design of the environment and learning material. According to this approach, educators in early education are not directors, but facilitators who carry out their work with discretion and humility. As Romano Guardini once said, "the corresponding mission of the educator is to allow the child to develop his own mode of being and to encourage him to get used to acting on his own initiative."[4]

Later on, during formal education, beginning at the age of six or seven, structure and discipline in learning will logically have increasingly more weight; but in children with internal drive, who are used to spontaneous discovery, the structure of direct instruction will not restrict, but rather introduce the conditions for wonder to operate. For example, a teenager will wonder at the beauty of a theorem if he or she has a grasp of mathematics. Wonder is not incompatible with the transmission of knowledge – in fact, wonder is *the desire to know*. Reality is the measuring stick of learning, and wonder is triggered by contact with its beauty, as we shall explore further in chapter 16.

It would be a mistake to take *spontaneous discovery* out of context and conclude that children should not have any limits imposed upon them. Montessori summed it up well when she said that the children in her schools do not do what they like, but they like what they do. The first and obvious limit in learning is that of reality: reality is discovered, not constructed. We agree, as social constructivists do, that our understanding of reality is developed through social interaction and in the light of previous knowledge, but neither the child nor the teacher can create reality, ontologically speaking. As Aquinas explains, "he who teaches does not cause the truth, but knowledge of the truth, in the learner. For the propositions which are taught are true before they are known, since truth does not depend on our knowledge of it, but on the existence of things."[5] Reality does not depend on us knowing it, nor does it depend on a teacher explaining it.

One way of combining discipline and invention is through *guided discovery*, in a *prepared environment*, as suggested by Montessori. It offers a minimal structure: the space where the children are; the materials that have been placed at their disposal; a few basic norms for using the materials, for reasons of order and ease of interaction; and a well-prepared guide who accompanies them. In this kind of environment, the children can be given free rein for discovery.

It is important that the toys we choose do not, as much as possible, have either batteries or buttons. The child's inner drive must provide these. It is not the toy that should function on its own, but rather the child who should put it into action through play. Children must have space for thought, without everything being spoon-fed to them. Contrary to what the mechanistic model argues, it is good that the questions our children ask be sometimes left without response.

Invention through play is especially important in the healthy development of children. Rules, methods and educational material are mere supports, never ends in themselves. Play is the activity *par excellence* through which small children learn, driven by wonder. In fact, some studies confirm that less-structured time helps children develop executive functions that are key to learning,[6] such as problem solving, creativity,[7] the capacity for sustained attention[8] and better control of their impulsiveness.[9] In an article published in the *Harvard Educational Review*, it was argued that children's intellectual development is primarily driven by their curiosity, a mechanism that sustains authentic learning.[10] Play is the ideal context in which children can give free rein to their curiosity.

A study carried out in 2011 found that creativity in children in preschool to junior school had decreased significantly in the last 20 years.[11] Many people have spoken of a crisis of creativity in the educational system and in society in general. Csikszentmihalyi, an expert on creativity, says that enjoyment of a task and the flourishing of creativity while one carries it out fall halfway between boredom and anxiety.[12] Boredom occurs when a task is too easy relative to the skill level of the person who carries it out; without challenge, there is no motivation. That is the reason why 40% of great creative thinkers, like Einstein, for example, were poor students.[13] Anxiety, by contrast, occurs when a task is too difficult for the skill level of the person who carries it out. The individual feels incapable and frustrated, and this stifles his or her ability to learn. This is the reason, for example, why children climb up a slide instead of sliding down it. It is not that they lack discipline; rather, they are looking for challenges that suit their abilities.

Activities that are too structured, or in which discipline takes priority over invention and discovery, pigeonhole small children into one of two states: boredom or anxiety. On the other hand, sources of fun and entertainment – films, video games, computers, smartphones, tablets, etc. – although they may supposedly be intended for educational purposes, make children more passive and distracted, since little mental effort is demanded of them, and thus the mind becomes idle and accustomed to not thinking. That is the reason we notice more and more bored children at earlier and earlier ages.

In guided discovery, by contrast, children naturally seek equilibrium between boredom and anxiety. Their innate desire to learn leads them to seek challenges that correspond to their abilities, to better understand their surroundings, and to develop their creative thinking. We must convince ourselves that playing is not a waste of time.

To discover in what situation our children find themselves in this respect, we can apply what I call the "Boredom Test". Vacations, holidays and weekends are good times for observing our children in the ideal *prepared environment*, where there are less-structured activities, and no external overstimulation. We can let them play freely for a couple of hours with their siblings, without toys, without trading cards, without screens, without bicycles, in open spaces in nature, and then watch to see how they cope. Do they entertain themselves on their own, quietly, imagining games, or do they get bored and experience anxiety and hyperactivity? It is not normal for children between three and six years old to get bored, because their creativity is infinite. When children get bored, it means that during the rest of the year they are conditioned by a frenzied pace of life, by an overly structured atmosphere, or by continuous artificial stimuli. If our children pass the Boredom Test out in nature, then we can repeat it in a waiting room at the dentist or the doctor – of course, in one that does not have screens, though such places have become scarce.

Discovery without guidance can lead to chaos, but guidance and discipline without discovery lead to the fulfillment of Carl J. Jung's prophecy: "We are all born originals and die copies." Children merely do what they are told – no more, no less. They learn to press buttons instead of imagining other ways of resolving situations. And when no one tells them what they are supposed to do, they look at the students beside them and imitate them so that they do not stand out and do not have to take responsibility for their decisions. The lack of inventiveness and discovery almost always ends in an unwillingness to take responsibility and an attitude of conformity.

7

Longing

Abundance, even of good things, prevents them from being valued.

Miguel de Cervantes

The most direct and efficacious way of extinguishing children's wonder is to give them everything they want, without even giving them the opportunity to long for it. A lack of limits or frenzied consumption by children destroys wonder because it causes them to take everything for granted: an attitude that is contrary to wonder. They think that things necessarily behave the way they themselves want them to. Or worse – they think that *people* must always behave the way they want them to.

Anything valuable takes time. A pregnancy, a pumpkin, a butterfly, friendship, love ... If we wait for them, we long for them, we recognise the effort they require, then we appreciate them more. We wonder at their very existence.

We have all witnessed a birthday party where the young host, whether our own child or another, opened his or her gifts mechanically – almost with indifference. This is because, faced with so many gifts, the child loses interest in them ... and so we enter into a downward spiral of consumerism where it takes more and more effort to dazzle the child, with things that are more and more sophisticated, and of course, more expensive.

An excess of things saturates the senses and does not give children a chance to long for anything. When children do not have the opportunity to long for something, they lose interest and it becomes necessary to entertain them from without using artificial stimuli:

fast-paced movies, smartphones, entertainment, violent video games, or whatever it may be. When what they have on hand is finished, they seek entertainment in breaking rules in order to provoke authority, whether at school, at home, or in other environments. It should be no surprise that an increasing number of children lend themselves to these rebellious "games" at an earlier and earlier age.

I once arranged an interview with a teacher of kindergarten who placed much emphasis on wonder in her classroom, and so I asked her if she saw a loss of wonder in the children over the last years. She understood me immediately and responded as follows:

> Definitely. And that has repercussions in learning. Children cannot learn if they don't have a sense of wonder. Without wonder, teachers have to put on a more and more elaborate act to ensure that children pay attention. For example, the other day, it was a special day at the school and we let them go for a walk in the woods nearby to have a picnic there. We wanted to take advantage of being there to use it as a learning opportunity. It was a way of calming them down because I saw that they were very restless. But it didn't interest them at all. It was like we had stayed in class. It made no difference to them whatsoever. This makes it very difficult to pass any knowledge on to them, because they absorb everything like a raincoat absorbs water. This loss of wonder has more repercussions. Children seek new sensations because everyday things no longer interest them. And since they don't find these in ordinary things, they start to seek them in breaking the rules. They go outside of the boundaries of the playground, break things, throw food in the lunch room, refuse to obey in the classroom, insult the teacher's aides, etc. It worries me a lot, because if this continues, they might do things that are much worse when they are teenagers . . .

"I'm forty and I *still* obey my parents, but my kids don't obey me!" a mother complained when faced with the thousand capricious desires of her children. What has happened so that we sacrifice our lives for the sake of luxuries and distractions for our children? It is true that many parents give in to the whims of their children because cultural pressure to have a "trophy child" is very strong nowadays. "You poor thing, you have to wear hand-me-down clothes from your older brother. You poor thing, you have to wear a backpack that is out of style at school. You poor thing, you have to wear old trainers until the end of the school year. You poor thing, you don't have the trendy trading cards that everyone has. You poor thing . . ." We are prepared to do anything for our child so that they never have less than another child, because we love them. But what our children need from us is our time and our unconditional attention, not the most recent model of an iPhone. However, the commercial and the social pressure is so high that we might end up, without being aware of this, converting our child into a trophy, as Carlo Honoré explains:

> Celebrity dads from David Beckham to Brad Pitt flaunt their kids like fashion accessories while pregnancy, once career suicide for an actress, has become the fastest route onto the front page of *Hello!* or *People*, with the paparazzi scrambling to snap the latest A-list baby. In several countries, surveys suggest that the very wealthy have started having larger families. Kids are now a status symbol, the ultimate possession in a consumerist culture. Never mind the trophy wife. This is the age of the trophy child.[1]

It is only one step from a trophy child to a tyrant child. From the parents' point of view, a trophy child is so perfect that he or she cannot be corrected. In order that such children appear quiet and well-behaved in public, parents must give in to their every whim. "Mum, give it to me or I'll make a scene that you won't forget," a mother senses her four-year-old child threatening at a social event. Anything is worth it to avoid a tantrum. We buy peace and quiet by putting chocolate biscuits and crisps in our children's lunches instead of a well-balanced meal, or avoid making demands on them so that it does not become evident how little authority we have over them. We maintain a clear conscience thanks to the hours we spend buying the necessary arsenal to keep them looking under control and well-behaved.

It is more and more normal to see children in the street who are simply crying out for limits, but in vain. Children who have never had someone tell them *no* right to the end, without giving in. They are children who know the rules and follow them well in order to achieve what they want. In the best of cases, they say "thank you" because they know the *magic word*, but are deeply ungrateful because we have allowed the seed of cynicism to germinate within them. They are children who fight, who shout, who break everything, who run without watching where they are going, who select their own clothing at the shops and from the wardrobe, who always complain about what they find on their plate, who devour an entire bag of Wotsits in thirty seconds, who open their birthday presents with boredom, who respond rudely to adults, who do not make eye contact, unless it be with a look of defiance . . . and all this, without suffering consequences. Under the passive gaze of parents who have thrown in the towel. Tyrant children. Would-be despots.

How can all of this be undone? There are many variables at play, but essentially, it can be achieved with more wonder: fewer luxury items and more unbranded products, fewer smartphones and more family time, fewer video games and more bicycle rides, fewer material rewards and more displays of affection, fewer television shows and more hikes in the mountains observing nature, fewer headphones and more times of silence; learning that the good and the valuable take time and effort; knowing how to distinguish between what our child asks for and what his nature calls for, which is not always the same, and, above all, knowing how to say no . . . right to the end.

Respecting children's spontaneous discovery within the framework of rules is not in itself a contradiction. On the contrary, we have already seen that discipline and discovery are complementary in a prepared environment that is conducive to spontaneous discovery within certain limits. Though it is true that sometimes one of children's favourite games consists in testing those limits, it is preferable not to play at this game. For example, how can one prevent children from removing the hats we have put on them to protect them from the sun? By putting them back on. What if they take them off again? Put them back on again. If they take them off again? Put them back on again. Until they stop taking them off. And if a child is old enough to foresee the consequences of his or her actions, we can return home, saying, "It's too bad, we can't go to the park because you don't wear your hat, and it's very sunny and I don't want you to get burned. Another day, maybe . . . what a shame!" It is better that they spend their time playing within the limits rather than testing them.

However, it is necessary to realise an important detail. Babies do not tease. Assuming that they do initiates a vicious circle of mistrust between them and their parents that intensifies feelings of neglect and their need to call attention to themselves. In fact, before the age of about two, children do not yet have the capacity to obey and it is preferable to remove a dangerous object from their reach rather than calling their attention to it every time they touch it. When they cry and complain, they are asking us to pay attention to them to resolve their basic physiological or emotional needs. We have to help them to regulate their habits such as sleeping and eating, without ignoring the need of babies to be cared for and without falling into a behaviourism that reduces them to mere passive subjects, "programmable" through external stimuli (rewards and punishments) that are aimed towards conditioning their behaviour.

From the age of about two, by which point children have established the basis for a secure attachment with their principal caregivers (and said attachment is precisely the consequence of having attended to their basic needs), children begin, gradually, to have the capacity to obey and we must help them to discover the natural consequences of their actions. They must begin to understand one of the most important laws of our world: ultimately we are free to make decisions, but are not free from the natural consequences our actions provoke. The world does not necessarily work the way we would like it to work. For example, children's tantrums, that are common at the age of two, are nothing other than a result of the frustration that arises when they realise this fact. "The world doesn't work the way I want it to, so I'll get angry to make sure it does." If we give in, we reinforce their false hope. If we do not give in, we make it clear that actions have natural consequences and that reality does not behave according to the whims of children. In this way, we help them to gain a sense of context, to re-establish contact with reality and accept its limits. The sooner they do so, the fewer tantrums we will be subjected to, and the less frustration they will feel when they begin to live with other people. The world has its laws. The sun burns, and if we do not protect ourselves, we get burned, whether we want it or not. Each family has its own rules and ways of doing things. If a child wants to go to the park on a sunny day and one of the child's parents says that he or she must wear a hat, but the child refuses, then he or she simply cannot go to the park. There is no need to present the rule as an imposition, or the consequences as punishments or blackmail, but rather as natural consequences of the child's actions so that he or she understands and accepts them. And if we deal with it cheerfully, without drama, and both parents agree on what the rules are, so much the better. Our children see our confidence and will not begin the game of testing limits. It is true that parents are not in an advantageous position to do so, because we lack time. Managing a tantrum well requires time. Educating requires time. And time can be difficult to come by.

Children whose senses are saturated by consumerism tend to be unappreciative; it will be harder for them to adapt to reality and to manage frustration. It is increasingly difficult for children who have everything to make the effort to achieve something good because they confuse what is good with the sensation of pleasure and wellbeing that they receive from the saturation of their senses. Aristotle, quoting Plato, said that right education consists in knowing how to delight in and suffer for the things that are valuable, and thus we ought to have been brought up this way from our youth.[2] Discovery arises naturally in children, because their desire to know naturally tends towards truth, goodness and beauty, as we shall see next. Nonetheless, this desire to know cannot spring up in chaos, in constant noise, in the saturation of the senses, in an environment without limits or discipline. What is good takes effort. Miguel de Cervantes said that "the path of virtue is very narrow, and the road to vice broad and spacious." Pampered, spoiled children who have not been given limits will be children with depleted willpower, with the wings of effort too short for them to achieve excellence, because excellence always comes at a price. It might seem paradoxical to speak of limits and effort as conditions for freedom, but it is not. Montessori resolved the apparent paradox with the following words:

'To let the child do as he likes,' when he has not yet developed any powers of control is to betray the idea of freedom. The result is children who are disorderly because order [has] been arbitrarily imposed upon them . . . Real freedom, instead, is a consequence of development . . . of the personality, reached by effort and one's own experiences.[3]

8

Nature

If a child never sees the stars, never has meaningful encounters with other species, never experiences the richness of nature, what happens to that child?

Richard Louv, *Last Child in the Woods*

It is a wholesome and necessary thing for us to turn again to the earth and in the contemplation of her beauties to know the sense of wonder and humility.

Rachel Carson, *Silent Spring*

Nature is one of the first sparks to light the flame of wonder in a child, and indeed is the spark that can allow someone who has lost a sense of wonder to recover it.

We recently planted tomatoes and strawberries in our little garden. The plants in question had dozens of promising flowers. With the children, we selected a partially shaded spot where we prepared the soil, buried the seedlings' roots, and watered them. The following day, my four-year-old son came running to see me and told me, in a grave tone:

"Mum, it didn't work. There are no tomatoes or strawberries."

"Tomatoes grow very slowly," I explained.

"Like me?"

"Yes, like you," I told him.

"Then it's going to take forever, Mum."

"Not quite, you just have to be patient."

Children have become accustomed to getting everything without effort and before they have a chance to long for it. Nowadays, I think that the only process that children see occurring at its natural pace – because it is one of the few we have not managed to speed up – is pregnancy. We need to patiently wonder more than ever, watching how a snail crawls, observing how a flower grows, how a drop of rain slides down the back of a fuzzy caterpillar, watching buds appear on a tree, watering plants, gathering mushrooms, feeding birds. Children must learn to raise their gaze skyward from time to time, as we used to do when we stretched out on the grass, which poked us and tickled us behind the legs and the ears, and imagined that the clouds took the shape of rabbits and dinosaurs. Children must return to the woods we ourselves visited when we were young, climb the trees, and hide behind the ferns or bushes. We must find those open spaces in nature where children can run, jump, discover, and imagine – not only on sunny days, but also on rainy days when the smell, the colours, the vegetation, and the little animals that allow themselves to be seen are different.

Perhaps this has not occurred to us because we think that it is not safe, because we are afraid of our children falling out of a tree, because they will get their new clothes dirty, because at best they will get scratched in the bushes, because we think that contact with flowers will trigger an allergic reaction, or because we believe that a walk in the rain will bring on a cold. It is strange that we parents seem to be afraid of nature sometimes – and if *we* are afraid, this fear will be passed on to our children. Why is it that children these days seem to run in fright at the first drop of rain? Why are they afraid of a little water and cold? Because there is a false popular belief that children catch colds and the flu when they are outside in the winter. "It is easier to smash an atom than a prejudice," Einstein said. The American Academy of Pediatrics tells us clearly that cold temperatures are never the cause of a cold or flu, despite the popular belief that leads us to believe the contrary. In fact, it tells us that if colds and the flu are more common in winter, it is because children spend less time outdoors, spending their day in classrooms where there is no ventilation and where they are in continual contact with each other, which facilitates the transmission of the virus.[1]

Thus, in order to fight against the common cold and the flu, and in doing so make children more resistant to frustration and difficulties, we have to let them run around outdoors, splashing in puddles with their rain boots – wrapped up in a sweater or two and a rain jacket, of course. This is typically the case in the majority of northern countries, where children play on the playground at -20°C. The good news is that this provides an excellent plan for rainy days, when we thought there was no alternative to placing our children in front of a screen, shut up at home or in class like caged lions.

Children have a natural affinity for nature. Perhaps this is because they are small, like the vast majority of the wonders that nature has to offer, as Rachel Carson suggests:

> Many children, perhaps because they themselves are small and closer to the ground than we, notice and delight in the small and inconspicuous. With this beginning, it is easy to share with them the beauties we usually miss because we look too hastily, seeing the whole and not its parts. Some of nature's most exquisite handiwork is on a miniature scale, as anyone knows who has applied a magnifying glass to a snowflake.[2]

Nature is capable of holding children's attention for hours, as they examine plants and insects, and play with mud and water. Studies demonstrate that playing in natural environments reduces the symptoms of attention deficit in some children. Nature permits our children to encounter reality in its pure state, teaching them that things do not come about instantly and that what is good and beautiful takes time. This helps them to become strong, patient, and able to control their impulsivity and to live with less in order to have more later – a quality that is clearly in short supply in today's children and youth.

Nature is also the first school where our children learn the natural laws of our world. Woodie Flowers, a professor of mechanical engineering at the Massachusetts Institute of Technology in Boston, and known for his contribution to the humanisation of technology, says that robots obey the laws of nature exactly, and when a robot breaks down, it is because it was constructed without taking these laws into account. He states that nature acts as an objective judge, providing the feedback that allows us to hit the mark when it comes to technology. He adds that students who take notice of nature as an objective judge develop a self-esteem founded on the truth of nature, which he calls a "robust" self-esteem.[3]

Antonio Gaudí, the brilliant architect of the Basilica of the Sagrada Familia in Barcelona, thought of nature as his teacher: "This tree close to my workshop is my mentor." Gaudí found his inspiration in the Beauty of the Divine; he was a profoundly spiritual man. But what life experience can allow a man to develop the genius necessary to undertake and develop a work of such magnificence? In the museum dedicated to Gaudí in Barcelona, one can find the following response:

> Antonio Gaudí . . . was in frail health from a young age, and his continuous attacks of rheumatism kept him from playing children's games and delayed his entry into elementary school. His mother spent many hours with him, entertaining him with walks in the countryside, observing nature. Recalling his childhood, Gaudí, then older, wrote: "With flowerpots surrounded by vines and olive trees, enlivened by the clucking of poultry, the chirping of birds, and the buzzing of insects, and with the Prades Mountains in the background, my mind captured the purest and most pleasant images of Nature, that Nature who will always be my Mentor."

Nature was the first thing to light the flame of wonder in Gaudí and was the inspiration for his masterpiece. Gaudí knew how to bring Beauty and the Divine to the streets and elevate the spirits of thousands of people heavenward through the wonder of the beauty of nature. Gaudí did not begin school early; he did not have talking toys, nor did he go to extracurricular mathematics courses twice a week, or to robotic summer school; nor did he watch Baby Einstein. He led a contemplative childhood in the company of his mother, and his best friend, silence, under the tutelage of his mentor, nature.

Thus, nature plays a more important role in the learning process of our children than we can imagine . . .

9

Pace and rhythms

Stop the world – I want to get off.

Leslie Bricusse and Anthony Newley

There was a merchant who sold special pills that quench thirst. You need only swallow one pill a week and you would no longer feel any need to drink.

"Why are you selling those?" asked the little prince.

"They are a wonderful time-saver," said the merchant. "Experts have made calculations. You can save fifty-three minutes in every week."

"And what do you do with those fifty-three minutes?"

"Anything you like . . ."

"As for me," said the little prince to himself, "if I had fifty-three minutes to spend, I would walk at my leisure toward a water fountain . . ."

Antoine de Saint-Exupéry, *The Little Prince*

From our point of view, children are slow. As slow as snails. Slow at getting dressed, slow at obeying, slow at understanding ("How many times have I told you to . . ."), slow at eating, slow at walking. So, so slow . . .

"Mum, when we're in the car, where should I be?" four-year-old Jane asked her mother.

"What do you mean, Jane?"

"Well, when we get home in the evening, you tell me that I

should be having supper. When I'm eating supper, you tell me I should be in the bath. When I get out of the bath, you tell me I should be brushing my teeth. When I'm brushing my teeth, you tell me I should be in bed. So, when we are in the car, where should I be?"

Fast and slow are very subjective concepts. Slow compared to what? We think of children as being slow because we are comparing their pace with ours – we tend to live in the "later", spending our entire life running after a goal without actually knowing where we are truly heading, while they live in and enjoy the present moment.

"What rotten luck. We're practically at a standstill. I can't believe this," Paul's father groaned, finding himself in a line of cars several kilometres long on the way to a hotel with a pool, tennis, ping-pong, great views, good service and exceptional cuisine where he planned to spend the weekend with his family.

"What's that?" Paul asked, pointing through the car window at an immense field of poppies.

"Those are poppies."

"And that?"

"That's wheat," his father replied, unable to conceal his deep disappointment at the situation.

On the way back home, Paul's father asked his children what they liked most about the weekend: the pool, ping-pong, the beach, the views, the hotel . . .?

"The wheat and the poppies," Paul responded.

Children live in the present with an impressive intensity. They do not live to fulfil obligations. They do not think in terms of schedules or checklists. They do not long for the past. They do not understand the concept of efficiency and do not live in "if-only-ness" or a constant state of regret. They enjoy the moment. To put it in the words of Heraclitus, "time is a game played beautifully by children."

Nowadays, it seems that we are swept away by the currents of a river of busyness whose destination we do not know. It seems as if it is always in motion. Children, on the other hand, have the key to happiness: living each moment of the present with intensity and wonder.

If we were to see things through the eyes of a four-year-old child, we would observe the following:

My father is shaking my shoulder while I am fast asleep and it is still very dark out. I would like to snuggle up in his arms while I wake up slowly, like I do on Sundays at my grandmother's house after my afternoon nap, but I cannot. He lifts me out of bed and begins to dress me hurriedly, repeating over and over again, "You have to be more independent." I am not sure what "independent" means. Then, I eat breakfast with my little brother. It is strange that my parents find the game of "let's see who can finish first" so interesting. I play because they find it exciting. While we play the game, I see that they burn their lips on their coffee and choke on their toast, often looking at the clock. They pick us up and load us into the car, because "there's no time" for us to walk. We get to the babysitter running, sometimes because "I'll be late for work!" other times because "I'm double-parked!" For each step my father takes, I have to take three, because my legs are shorter. Once, I told my parents I had to go pee when we were in the car on the way to school, and they got very angry. I do not know why. Is it bad to have to go pee? But the worst was the day when my mother found out I had a fever before putting me in the car. My parents put their hands on their head and there was a long moment of silence. They gave me medicine and took me to the babysitter. In the middle of the morning, my babysitter called my mother; my aunt came to get me and took me to my grandmother's house. I was very happy then, because my grandmother took care of me.

"Children must be very understanding of grown-ups," said the little prince. Children have their own rhythms: the biological ones of sleeping and eating; intellectual ones for learning and understanding;

and emotional ones: they need hugs, they want to be listened to, and they want to be seen with compassion and affection. Their rhythms are certainly not ours. When we want to satisfy some need of theirs, at best they do not need it at that exact moment. That is why it is not sufficient to provide attention at regular intervals: we must also be *available* to resolve the basic needs of our children as they arise. Adults must rediscover the sensitivity that nature has conferred upon them and that has been extinguished through the circumstances of a harried and sometimes hysterical life. We must re-learn to harmonise the attention we give our children with their rhythms in such a way that they can perceive the sense of the consequences of their own actions. It is true that children need us to set limits and guide them in their development, but before placing demands on them, we must satisfy their basic needs.

Children have an internal clock and they themselves – not what they demand, but what their nature demands – are the measure of what they need. Not the schedule we adults follow. For example, detecting what time children start falling asleep at night, and always putting them to bed before then, assures us that they will sleep the amount of time necessary to be able to wake up well rested, which is key for their mental and physical health.‡

Studies associate a lack of sleep in children with hyperactivity, lack of mental flexibility, difficulty in controlling impulsiveness, behavioural problems and a reduction in cognitive ability, in addition to difficulties in managing emotions and adapting to certain circumstances.[1] We also know that sleep is necessary for the consolidation of what we learn throughout the day.

One must take into consideration the fact that the time our children are in bed and the time they actually fall asleep may be

---

‡ According to the National Sleep Foundation of the United States (http://www.sleepfoundation.org), children need to sleep, according to their age, the following amount of time in a period of 24 hours: 0–2 months: 10.5–18 hours; 3–11 months: 9–12 hours during the night (plus 0.5–2 hours of napping, 1–4 times a day); 1–3 years: 12–14 hours (including a 1–3-hour nap); 5–12 years: 10–11 hours.

different, especially when they must manage academic requirements and demanding extracurricular activities. Various studies associate the habit of being in front of a screen with difficulties falling asleep and with sleep disorders, so that the American Academy of Pediatrics recommends that there be no digital media in bedrooms and that children avoid consuming such media within an hour of going to bed.[2]

Our children need to sleep as much as their nature demands, not as much as we sleep. Our children also need a balanced diet. Paediatricians never tire of repeating this. They need baby food without salt, fruit without sugar, fewer processed pastries, fewer sweets, and no caffeine at all. Caffeine is a psychoactive substance. Unfortunately, we find cola drinks within their reach at the vast majority of birthday parties and in the refrigerators of many households. Sometimes we give in because of a lack of time. Educating our children on the necessity of a good diet takes time and extra effort.

Paying attention to the rhythms and basic necessities of our children is key to ensuring their healthy development. More than a decade of investigation on children's attachment patterns confirms that children who perceive their basic needs – emotional, physiological, etc. – being attended to in the first years of life will have more balanced emotions, will be more sure of themselves, and will be better disposed for learning. Children who have been properly taken care of receive the message "I'm worth the effort", which has positive repercussions on their self-esteem because what we are telling them indirectly is that they are competent individuals.

To respect the pace and rhythms of children is also to respect the stages of their development without trying to accelerate or rush them. They need us to respect the pace of their cognitive and emotional development, to protect their innocence, without giving in to the temptation to shorten their childhood.

10

Hyper-education: The "Baby Einstein" generation

When milestones become millstones.

Carl Honoré, Under Pressure

*The years of early childhood are the time to prepare the
soil. Once the emotions have been aroused – a sense of the
beautiful, the excitement of the new and the unknown, a
feeling of sympathy, pity, admiration or love – then we wish
for knowledge about the object of our emotional response.
Once found, it has lasting meaning. It is more important to
pave the way for the child to want to know than to put him
on a diet of facts he is not ready to assimilate.*

Rachel Carson, The Sense of Wonder (1956)

Respecting our child's sense of wonder is incompatible with hyper-education. Hyper-education is the obsession with accelerating children's cognitive and emotional development so that they become *superchildren*. It consists in converting the milestones in a child's life into a veritable relay race.

The other day, my son was invited to a classmate's birthday party. I could not believe it. The parents had hired a professor to present chemistry experiments for eight-year-old children. It seems that clowns have already gone out of style . . .

How far are we prepared to go to prepare the way for our child's professional future? How many of us parents have fallen into the dangerous trap of excitement at the thought that we might have the next Einstein or Michael Jordan in the family? Cue the extracurricular activities: Kumon maths, piano, Mandarin, tennis . . . As soon as their children can lift their heads up, some parents put them in an easy chair to watch *Baby Einstein*™, one of the most hypnotising children's cartoon series, which enjoyed international fame because it was supposedly "beneficial for children's development". When the Baby Einstein Company was asked to prove the educational merit of its products, it was unable to do so. Moreover, when a group threatened to sue the company on account of studies that related early exposure to television with potential negative effects, it retracted its statements and offered to issue refunds to all discontented parents. Nevertheless, *Baby Einstein*™ can still be found in many homes, or in preschools, which claim to use it for educational purposes.

More stimuli, introduced as early as possible, do not lead to better results. The majority of experts agree that children begin to have the intellectual maturity necessary for abstract thinking at the age of six. When we attempt to accelerate children's learning, asking them to do what their nature is not yet prepared to do, we place them in a situation of frustration that could have repercussions on their self-esteem and create a downward spiral of failure, which can affect their future learning development.

Early childhood is a period of preparation, during which less-structured time is key, because it allows children to develop executive functions that are necessary for learning, such as working memory, attentional control and planning.[1] Thus, parents do not have to be concerned when their children cannot write their name at the age of three or read at the age of four. Einstein himself, who did not begin learning to read or write until he was eight years old, saw this clearly. At one point, Thomas Edison asked Einstein about the speed of sound, to which Einstein replied:

I do not know. I do not carry such information in my mind since it is readily available in books. The value of college education is not the learning of many facts but the training of the mind to think, and in this way come to know something that is not found in books.

However, we continue to find ourselves with the paradigm that we have to bombard children with stimuli from the time they are born, in order to make them great.

"Your daughter needs to improve her drawing skills," a teacher said to the parents of one of her students. "At four years old, children shouldn't be drawing people floating in the air; they should be drawing people with their feet on the ground." The parents did not know what to think; they did not see that as a problem.

I do not know where Spanish art would be if Picasso and Dalí's parents had insisted on them reaching the curious milestone set by that good and well-intentioned teacher.

The obsession with making high achievers out of our little children means that in a preschool environment we fragment reality at an age when children are still not prepared to understand it, making various specialists file past them throughout the day to teach them music, languages, mathematics, etc. Programme divisions in early childhood are also contrary to the unity of a child's life. The entire universe as a whole is constituted, for children, by what they perceive through sensory experiences. The scientific distinctions and classifications made for adults do not fit with children's interior unity; instead they fragment their world.

As long as the heads and agendas of children are occupied by extracurricular activities, mounds of homework and goals of all sorts, they do not have time to think of what really suits them in this very precious stage of childhood: being with their loved ones, playing, imagining, discovering things on their own, without hurry . . . They need to draw people floating in the air, to run in a field chasing butterflies and picking wild flowers, to imagine fantastic adventures and secret passageways. The last thing a child needs is to spend the month of July sitting in the kitchen at home "filling the summer workbook", in order to put a tick in the right box instead of thinking outside it.

The rush to accelerate development also occurs in the realm of affectivity, when parents are afraid of their children being left behind in their maturity and turn to every technique of hyper-education, including the most far-fetched, to accelerate their passage from childhood to adulthood.

> Not long ago, I was told that a group of preschoolers was taken to a "museum of fear". The objective? To provoke a "controlled" fear in them in order to accelerate their psychological maturation. A psychologist, hired to relieve the anxiety of reticent parents, came to the preschool. And then on with the field trip! I do not know how the story ended; how many children cried and how many not; how many had nightmares and how many not; or what the average percentage of increase in maturity was.

We cannot forget that childhood is a step prior to adulthood that must be lived fully in order for the process to occur naturally. Romano Guardini warned of the consequences of accelerating development: "It is possible that the phase [of life] in question be oriented so much toward the next that it cannot develop its proper nature."[2]

11

The disappearance of childhood

Look how handsome you are with this haircut, buddy.
You're going to get all the ladies.

Our children's ex-hairdresser to my four-year-old son

In this patchwork of uniformity into which we insist on
shoehorning children, to force equality between children
and parents by erasing divisions between generations,
devaluing spontaneous discovery activities, determined
to restrictively program leisure time, with this eagerness
to suppress bursts of creativity and genius in children . . .
we are killing the child. Maybe we do not realize it, but it
is now time to urgently reflect and seek solutions to this
unpunished massacre.

Paulino Castells, child neuro-psychiatrist

Childhood must be lived in its turn, with everything wonderful that it entails: imagination, play, a sense of mystery, innocence, etc. Skipping over stages of childhood depreciates the mechanism on which nature counts in order to ensure a healthy development of the personality. Childhood is like chicken pox. If one does not get it when one is young, it is manifested as a more serious illness when one is older; as a condition called *childishness*: the attitude of an adult that is reflected in the following anecdote, as reported by a parent:

The other day, I saw a father teaching his son the different brands of cars in a parking lot. "That one is a Ford. That's a Volkswagen and it's better. That's an Audi, which is better than a Volkswagen. And that is a BMW, which is also better than a Volkswagen. Then there's the Ferrari, but there aren't any here, and I've already taught you about them."

Another parent recounted the following:

"Recently, my six-year-old son played a game of naming car brands in class. Those who did not know them were eliminated. The one who knew the most won."

How many categories of healthier and more interesting things are there in the world that could be used in this game? Being "eliminated" in front of twenty other children for not knowing car brands at the age of six, in addition to having little educational value, introduces into the school environment a new reality: *brand bullying*, ever more present in the playground. Children spend hours and hours comparing what they have with what other people have, from trainers to remote-control cars to socks . . . These negative cycles promote "brandism" and introduce a reality into the world of a child that does not belong, and should not belong, to his or her stage of life.

We expect children to comply with our own way of thinking. But why? On one hand, the images that reach children from the world of marketing are more and more invasive, and they are only a click away from them. Furthermore, children are often portrayed as little adults: they appear on magazine covers, in commercials, in television shows, with a casual and cynical attitude. Children strike sensual poses whose significance they do not yet understand, and wear clothing that is not suitable for their age, to the point that it seems at times that they have been converted into objects of desire: trophy children. On the other hand, the pressure of the competitive and demanding world and the innate desire that all parents have for their children's success leads them to want to instil in them, as soon as possible, a set of behaviours and knowledge without necessarily realising that these do not fit with the process of maturation and the interior order of the child's inner life. In short, there is an inexplicable eagerness nowadays to leapfrog stages of development, so that children exhibit characteristics proper to adults – in the way they dress, eat, entertain themselves, speak, and even walk.

We are witnessing the "disappearance of childhood", which consists of frustrating children's need to play, killing their imagination and enthusiasm and thereby shortening childhood – that sacred stage of life. Bob Samples wrote that: "Albert Einstein once spoke of intuition as a sacred gift and likened rationality to a faithful servant. Our basic purpose was to shift the tendency to worship the servant and ignore the sacred."[1] Killing children's imagination, wonder and creativity in order to instil in them a rational attitude as soon as possible, and contrary to their nature, is typical of a cold, cynical and calculating society. This is contrary to wonder, of course.

We have taken the child out of childhood. We have converted children into little adults before their time. We have lost our sense of modesty in our behaviour and in conversations in their presence; we have let them watch what they should not see; we have taken away their fear of the horrible and their distaste for violence; and we have wrongly expected our children to mature before they are ready and in ways that demonstrate a misunderstanding of childhood.

The result? Children who have "seen and done it all"; who are not surprised or interested by anything, because everything is a click or a tap of the finger away, and thus they do not have a chance to long for it. Children left to play with a touch screen from the age of two, their delicate little fingers discovering damaging images that are forever engraved in their innocent minds. Cynical children who have shot and killed tens of thousands of times in video games; who have lost all sensitivity; who no longer have the ability to interpret a facial expression or to be courteous and attentive to others. Children without a sense of wonder, who have become blind to the beauty of reality, incapable of "tuning in" to it. Children enslaved by fads and "norms" of beauty that set them up for eroded self-esteem, or even anorexia. Children with heavy school bags and an agenda so full that they are like little stressed-out executives, burdened with a sea of obligations and activities. Children who have never had time to splash in a puddle or to create logistical chaos for a colony of ants, but who have seen more pornography than teenagers of previous generations who secretly and with difficulty procured some magazines.

It is no coincidence that endocrinologists warn of the tendency for an early onset of puberty, that shortening of childhood, which favours a lengthening of adolescence. It is strange that we parents are in such a hurry for our children to join us in a stage of life that we find so terrifying. It is also strange that the distinction between generations becomes ever more blurred over the course of one's life, not only in childhood. The famous designer Carolina Herrera said that nothing ages a woman more than dressing as if she were young. What a shame that so few people accept old age for what it is: something beautiful and natural. Every stage of life has a beauty of its own, and not simply in relation to other stages. No, children are not simply little, immature adults. Until they are ready to move on, in a natural way, to the next stage of life, it is children that they are and will remain.

12

Silence

*Without silence, there cannot be any real appreciation
in life, which is as delicate in its inner fabric as a closed
rosebud.*

Deepak Chopra

*It takes two years to learn to speak and sixty to learn to
keep quiet.*

Ernest Hemingway

Studies in neuroscience tell us that when we carry out various tasks at
once, we cannot pay attention to them all equally, but rather oscillate
rapidly between one and the other. That is the main reason why, for
instance, phone use is restricted while driving. It also explains why
some studies have demonstrated that having the television on continuously in a room can interrupt children's play,[1] or negatively influence
the quality of the interaction of parents with their children.[2] When we
receive an overload of stimuli from various sources, we do not process them all simultaneously, but instead divide our attention among
them. Consequently, when Emma pays attention to her smartphone
while she does her homework, with background music, in front of a
computer screen where a multitude of windows connect her live to
her favourite social networks and her email accounts, she is not more
intelligent, but rather suffers a decrease in her capacity to concentrate
on any one of the activities she is carrying out. In reality, she is not
carrying out any activity, but is instead passively receiving external
noise that she is managing on the fly without much thought.

Consequently, Emma, like other adolescents of her age, not only has a lesser capacity for concentration, but also less capacity to enjoy the present moment, less intuition in regards to the needs of others, and less sensitivity to silent or less noisy stimuli, like the smile her mother gives her while passing by her side, a fine rain beating on the roof, or the drumming of a woodpecker outside her bedroom window. Emma sees what surrounds her, but with nothing more than a superficial gaze. She passively receives information, but does not have an active attitude of expectancy in regards to it. The continuous noise leads to her not having her own inner life, which is why being alone with herself becomes intolerable and she goes in search of noise and new sensations in order to alleviate that feeling of emptiness. Events and her environment take control of her. This leads her to ask her teacher to motivate her, because she has become a spectator, rather than taking the leading role in her life.

With so much stimulation, such an invasion of foreign noise, wonder is suffocated and it becomes difficult for children, and then teenagers, to internalise what they learn, to deepen their knowledge, listen, receive, be attentive to the needs of others, make eye contact, think about the consequences of their actions, discern, ponder, reflect on the meaning of what they are doing . . . In order to reverse the damage, these children or teenagers must rediscover silence. It will not be an easy task, as silence is deafening for an overstimulated individual. For this reason it is recommended that one begins to prepare quiet spaces for children from a young age, keeping them away from environments that will daze them – performances, music, fast-paced visual stimuli, etc. – because these do not respect their rhythms. In short, it is important to prepare an environment for children that has a proper balance of silence, speech, images and sound. We parents and educators will know how to do this if we ourselves learn, through silence, how to listen for what our children's nature requires in any given moment. It is a curious fact that the spread of the ADHD epidemic coincides with the exponential increase in the use of technologies in childhood. We can further note that, in spite of the increased accessibility to so much information, we are increasingly concerned that children do not learn at the expected pace. Romano Guardini had already warned of this:

Knowledge and intellectual possession and dominion are increasing, in such an incommensurable measure that it literally overwhelms men ... but this deepness that blossoms from interior insight weakens, in look and experience, understanding of the essential, perception by the whole, experience, and meaning. And all of this can be obtained in the interior confrontation of contemplation; and it requires calm, rest, and concentration.[3]

Of course, silence is a variable that has been forgotten in the process of learning. Let us revisit Einstein's formula:

$$A \, (success) = X \, (work) + Y \, (play) + \mathbf{\textit{Z (keeping your mouth shut)}}$$

Silence is a very important part of learning and is necessary for reflection, one of the qualities that characterise the human person. Without silence, a person has denied and expelled from oneself that which is most proper to one: namely, that one is a being who thinks. Noise not only deafens, but also silences questions that arise out of a wonder that comes from observing reality. In order to learn, not only is it necessary to receive information, but it is necessary to assimilate and internalise it. And in order for this to happen, there must be quiet spaces: "keeping one's mouth shut", as Einstein says. The 21st-century equivalent of this advice would be to turn off digital devices.

There is also a relationship between silence and our children's capacity for obedience. Obedience cannot be reduced to *doing what someone else asks "just because"*. At some point I heard about a lecture series entitled "10 Techniques to Get Your Kids to Obey". The title implies, at the very least, a mechanistic approach. In order for children to be prepared to obey, two indispensable conditions must be met from the children's point of view: 1) the person asking them to do something has a trusting relationship[§] with them; 2) the children *know how to listen, from an inner silence*. When these two conditions

---

§   A trusting relationship is the same as the secure attachment mentioned previously; see footnote †, page 16.

are met, we can then expect obedience. It is true that we can *polish* the way we make demands on our children, but these two conditions come first. On the other hand, if children are dazed by, and saturated with noise, then they are incapable of managing, not to mention processing, more external demands. Whatever punishment is imposed on children who disobey without both conditions being met is counterproductive. Children will receive it as an act of aggression and will respond impulsively.

If then, in view of everything we have explained above, silence is so important, why do we surround our children with screens all day?

Taking a look at a magazine on new technologies "for the 21st-century classroom", one can find the following advertisement for children as young as four years old:

> One of the most remarkable devices that integrates the ActivClassroom concept is, without doubt, the interactive ActivTable ... This special table offers one of the largest screens on the market: no less than 46 inches ... Additionally, they can work on it, making use of its individual library, which includes keyboards, web navigation, and math tools ... Another feature ... is the interactive digital whiteboard ActivBoard 500 Pro, which stands out because of its inclusion of multi-touch technology that allows students to work simultaneously on its surface ... Additionally, it is equipped with an integrated sound system. ActivExpression2 is a response system for students that allows them to write complete answers to questions their teacher asks them: thanks to the QWERTY keyboard it incorporates, they can respond with complete sentences, numbers, symbols, mathematical equations, true/false, and much more. Additionally, its wide, backlit screen and similar design to a Smartphone, make it very intuitive and easy to use ... As for ActivEngage, students can use what it offers to contribute to class and answer questions in real time from its laptops, tablets, or handheld mobile devices. The teacher shows a question on the classroom screen (usually an IWB) using ActivInspire software from Promethean and students respond with a

click of the mouse on their PC on the answer they think is correct.[4]

Apart from the investment – or the spending – that such an arsenal involves for any school, it feeds parents' hope in Baby Einstein and the false belief in "the earlier, the more, the better", so that they think their children will be left behind if a tablet is not put into their hands when they are scarcely two, three or four years old. Our children will not miss the technological boat because it cannot be lost. It goes by every second! And at the speed at which everything advances, each "boat" of new technologies that goes by is obsolete after it has travelled 500 metres. The vast majority of new technologies that exist when a child is three years old will very probably not exist when he or she enters secondary school, or university, or the workforce, meaning that what one introduces to him or her at the age of three can be considered a waste of time. In the best of cases it will be considered "vintage." To use that first Motorola the size of a shoe was not an indispensable requirement for us to learn to use an iPhone almost instantaneously. The fact that children intuitively learn how to manage technology does not tell us that they are smarter than we were; the smart ones are the engineers who are designing it so they can be used in a "plug and play" mode. And navigating the internet in ten years' time, if it is still done the way it is now, will take thirty seconds to learn, when our children have sufficient maturity to manage the time they spend doing it, to filter content, to understand the concept of privacy, and to organise information based on previously acquired criteria founded on first knowing the world through contact with real people, in real situations, in the real world.

In fact, some senior executives of multinational technology companies established in Silicon Valley send their children to elite schools that pride themselves on not using technology in their classrooms.[5] Their parents work for eBay, Google, Apple, Yahoo, and Hewlett-Packard. Yet their children have never used Google . . . They write with pencil and paper and their teachers use a traditional blackboard. There is not a single screen in the entire school, and the school discourages screen use at home. The reason? Computers inhibit critical thinking, dehumanise learning and human interaction, and shorten the attention span of students. One of the parents, a Mr Eagle, a graduate in computer science who works in executive communications at Google, says:

> The idea that an app on an iPad can better teach my kids to read or do arithmetic, that's ridiculous . . . Technology has its time and its place . . . It's super easy. It's like learning to use toothpaste. At Google and all these places we make technology as brain-dead easy to use as possible. There's no reason why kids can't figure it out when they get older.

Steve Jobs is well-known for having been a low-tech parent.[6] Also, according to a recent *New York Times* article, Silicon Valley parents are growing increasingly concerned about the effects of technology on their children's development, to the point that they are asking their nannies to sign contracts guaranteeing zero screen exposure for their kids.[7] As a result of these parents' increasing panic over the impact screens have on their children, another article discusses their move towards screen-free lifestyles and worries over a "new" digital divide. It explains that the implementation of tablets in Silicon Valley is usually done in public schools, while private schools do not use them. It could happen that the children of poorer and middle-class parents will be raised by screens, while the children of Silicon Valley's elite will be going back to wooden toys and the "luxury of human interaction". It concludes that the digital divide is not what was expected.[8]

Recent studies show that the "digital native" concept lacks scientific basis. According to this "hypothesis", digital natives would have cognitive advantages that positively affect their learning, over the generation that precedes them. For example, they would have an advantage in technological multitasking.

Despite its popularity, this concept was questioned in several studies since 2008. Specifically, a report published in 2011 by various scholars found that the characteristics attributed to the digital natives have been overestimated.[9] While acknowledging that "young people demonstrate an apparent ease and familiarity with computers", it also found that: "they rely heavily on search engines, view rather than read and do not possess the critical and analytical skills to assess the information that they find on the web". In conclusion, the report overturns the common assumption that the "Google generation" is the most web-literate.

In 2017, a literature review on the concept of the "digital native" concluded that it lacks scientific basis.[10] The belief that a person born in the technological era has a greater ability to cognitively process multiple sources of information simultaneously is a myth. Although it is true that the human being has a great ability to adapt to its environment, an overly simplistic application of the brain plasticity concept in the educational context can lead to misinterpretation.

Without trying to demonise new technology – whoever speaks in these terms has understood very little of what is at stake when attempting to postpone its use in childhood – we have to be very cautious with anything that suffocates wonder, that drive that comes from within children and makes them question, take interest, imagine, search, discover, invent . . . in short, that makes them able to think, which is a quality that characterises us as human beings.

One activity that is carried out in exterior silence is reading, as Nicholas Carr describes in "Is Google Making Us Stupid? What the Internet is doing to our brains":

> In the quiet spaces opened up by the sustained, undistracted reading of a book, or by any other act of contemplation, for that matter, we make our own associations, draw our own inferences and analogies, foster our own ideas.[11]

Before being carried away by software and hardware that has struck them dumb by doing everything for them, and before giving in to the addictive habit of flitting like a butterfly from app to app and from website to website, our children must strengthen their reading habits. Reading, in order to have an inner life, capacity for critical thought, for reflection, for contemplation, for wonder. Reading . . . that is the boat they must board, and that we cannot allow them to miss, because it does not often stop later in life and it can take them a great distance.

13

Rituals

"What's a rite?"

[. . .]

"It's what makes one day different from the other days, one hour from the other hours."

The fox to the little prince, Antoine de Saint-Exupéry, The Little Prince

Wonder gives meaning to routine. What is routine? It is the repetition of useful, structured actions, which are sometimes timed and supervised. Sometimes it is necessary for the purpose of introducing order into a group, a family or a classroom, or to give children a sense of security through being able to anticipate what comes next. Whether we want it or not, life largely consists of a series of repeated actions. We all get up, shower, get dressed, have breakfast, commute to work, eat, return home, have dinner, and sleep for a few hours, until we wake up and repeat our routine, every day.

Routine is not in itself a bad thing. In fact, according to Montessori, repetition is the secret to children's perfection. But the kind of perfection that Montessori refers to is defined as the result of obeying the natural laws of childhood, not the arbitrary diktats of society. But can *any* repetition lead to perfection? Repetition without meaning can alienate children – and us as well – when it becomes an end in itself. It leads children to act mechanically, without being conscious of what they are doing, without seeing meaning, without putting heart, emotion and intelligence into it, and without internalising what they do and learn. In mechanical repetition, rather than being a personal subject, children become objects. Thus, the result of this process would be shaped by rigidity and limitation, rather than creativity and imagination. The kind of habit involved in this situation would be the result of coercion, mere inertia, training or perhaps addiction, but not of education.

In *Hamlet*, Shakespeare spoke of custom as a monster that consumes "all sense". Routine with meaning is something different. Let us call it *ritual*. When the little prince asks the fox what a rite is, the fox responds, "It's what makes one day different from the other days, one hour from the other hours."

Why do children find such satisfaction in sharing the repetition of actions that are apparently without significance? Waving to Dad when he drops them off at day care in the morning; pushing their nose against the window the same way every day while they say goodbye; letting their mother tickle them as she dries them after their daily bath; letting her help them jump out of their car seat, grabbing them by the hand and counting "one, two . . . three!", rekindling their excitement day after day; letting their father tickle them with his beard before he puts them to bed, and after the story they listen to, for the hundredth time with the same excitement every night. For children, time does not pass. It is they who pass through life.

What specifically makes the difference between routine that alienates children and ritual that they find so interesting and meaningful? Simply put, ritual *is* routine, but *humanised*.

Children experience wonder because they associate ritual moments with their loved ones, with their classmates, with their siblings, with their grandparents . . . it is what makes routine more human and gives it meaning, and it is what makes children wonder, what makes them desire to know what surrounds them.

The fox explains to the little prince that rituals can transform the monotony of life into an occasion of wonder:

My life is very monotonous . . . I hunt chickens; men hunt me. All the chickens are just alike, and all the men are just alike. And so I am a little bored. But if you tame me, it will be as if my life were filled with sunlight. I will know the sound

of footsteps that are different from all the others. Other footsteps send me hurrying back underneath the ground. Yours
will call me out of my burrow, like music. And then look!
You see the grain-fields over there? I do not eat bread. Wheat
is useless to me. The wheat fields remind me of nothing. And
that is sad! But you have hair that is the colour of gold. It will
be wonderful when you have tamed me! The grain, which is
also golden, will make me think of you. And I will love the
sound of wind in the wheat . . .[1]

The association of the repetition of an action or event with the
presence of a loved one is what humanises routine and transforms it
into a rite. And in childhood, the human dimension is key for learning.

14

The educator as a base for exploration

If a child is to keep alive his inborn sense of wonder . . .
he needs the companionship of at least one adult who can
share it, rediscovering with him the joy, excitement and
mystery of the world we live in.

Rachel Carson, *The Sense of Wonder*

Some years ago, a well-known newspaper in Barcelona made a list of the most repeated sentences in the city's parks. The one that was repeated the most was "Look, Mum!". There is nothing unusual about this, because children interpret the world around them using the person who loves them and in whom they trust as a base for exploration. This is how they learn. If we pay attention to six-month-old babies, we see that when they are carried by their mother towards a stranger, they look first at the stranger, then at their mother, then again at the stranger, and once more at their mother. It is as if they are asking permission, or as if they are looking at the unknown through the eyes of their principal caregiver. This process is well known and studied in psychology under the name "joint attention". When children discover something new, they need to share it with their parents in order to find meaning in it, to incorporate it into their pre-existent mental schemas. This process may even be silent: it happens through a discreet glance into the eyes of their mother, father or principal caregiver. They look through the eyes of those who take care of them and see reality through their eyes. In fact, when something out of the ordinary happens to our child, the first thing he or she will do is to look at us. If we look frightened, our child will be afraid. If we look upset, our child will be upset. If we laugh, he or she will find it amusing. This natural habit children have of looking through the eyes of their parents is the most powerful means we have for educating them. The environment is a determining factor in influencing the way they behave, but what they perceive that we, as educators, understand and think of this environment is even more powerful. Yes, the way we look at the world around us very much affects our children, whether we want it to or not. As Siegel says, "More important than sensory stimulation in the early years of development, however, are the patterns of interaction between child and caregiver." It is well known that children's curiosity unfolds through social interaction established with their principal caregiver. As Robert Fulghum says, "Don't worry that children never listen to you; worry that they are always watching you."[1]

We said before that educators – parents, teachers, etc. – are mediators and that the true agent of learning is the child. But this does not mean that educators have no importance at all. In fact, their role is key for learning. In early childhood, the educators are those who discreetly design children's environments and are a base for exploration, mediating between children's sensory experiences and their interpretation of these experiences. Educators serve as a reference point for a young child's exploration of the world: they are facilitators of meaningful learning. Later on, when the child enters into the stage of formal education, the educator's role must adapt to the child's new circumstances. The child is then ready for more abstract and complex knowledge, and this must sometimes be exposed in an orderly way, through teacher-directed instruction, understanding and adapting to the child's previous knowledge and to what he or she is able to understand at a given time. At that point, educators must be experts in helping children go through the process that some have described as "scaffolding". When children learn something new, they need to contextualise and assimilate it. They need to fit this piece of the puzzle into what they know, into their pre-existing knowledge. The intermediary figure of the educator is key to helping them make sense of this "fit".

In effect, the learning process is similar to the construction of scaffolding. As we explained earlier, children build on their pre-existing knowledge. Children construct their scaffolding, *but they cannot design it*. Here is where the role of a good teacher comes into play; a teacher who knows that before learning multiplication, one must know how to add, and that at the age of two, it is better to play than to learn addition. A good teacher knows that observing the fall of a leaf is the prelude to an interest in gravity. A good teacher knows that the beauty of a theorem can only be seen when a child has been given a previous understanding of mathematics that allows him or her to understand the theorem and see its beauty. And studies confirm that, in more formal stages of education, this knowledge acquisition cannot rely exclusively on a pure discovery approach; that the discovery approach – also called inquiry-based instruction – has to be combined with teacher-directed instruction.[2] All of this is an art; an art whose only artist is a sensitive educator. It is a shame that one cannot easily recognise the importance of sensitivity without already being truly sensitive.

However, given the technological age we are in, there is a current trend in education that tends to give more importance to methodologies, apps and devices than to the content and the teacher. What should we think of this? A McKinsey study,[3] published in 2007, compared 25 very successful educational systems from countries with varying levels of investment in education and asked what they had in common. The study concluded: "The quality of an education system cannot exceed the quality of its teachers."

Why? Because the teacher is the one who is capable of sensing, through the open eyes of a child, all the possibilities that the personal existence of each human being offers; the teacher is the one who loves and knows his or her material well and knows how to transmit it with passion, intuition and sensitivity, qualities that digital technologies – no matter how much Silicon Valley is willing to spend on them – will never have.

With this in mind, we now understand why young children are not moved by stories on CD. Perhaps we purchase them because we lack the time to read to our children, but they remain in their cases. It is for the same reason that studies demonstrate that infants do not learn words or other languages with DVDs, however educational they might be. There might, however, be benefits in relation to learning for specific content after the age of two when adults act as intermediaries between children and stories.[4]

There is also important evidence supporting a "video deficit effect" whereby infants and toddlers will suffer a learning deficit when a DVD is used for learning, as opposed to a live demonstration. This is due to the difficulty they experience in transferring new learning from a 2D representation to a 3D reality.[5]

This is why it is so important that the intermediary between our little children and the world they discover be a person who loves them – *not a screen*.

Furthermore, in so far as we act as mediators between our children and what they discover in their first years of life, we will then be in a privileged situation to be credible to them when they enter their teenager years, as explains Dorothy Canfield Fisher, in 1914:

> If, hand in hand with them, she has sought out the reason why milkweed seeds have down on them and why a three-legged stool will stand firmly on uneven ground, it is most likely that when the moment comes for an inquiry into the darker mysteries and disappointments of life, she may have the poignant satisfaction of feeling her child's hand reach out instinctively and grasp hers in the hour of trial. And no greater reward than this can crown the efforts of a mother's life.[6]

15

The meaning of mystery

The most beautiful thing we can experience is the mysterious. It is the source of all true art and science.

Albert Einstein

"Mum, how does the fairy find out when kids lose their teeth?"

"I don't know," the mother responded, caught off guard by her seven-year-old daughter's surprise question. "I guess mothers must tell them, I don't know."

"Have you ever talked to the tooth fairy, Mum?" the girl asked excitedly.

"No, no, never!"

"So how did the tooth fairy find out?" the little girl repeated.

"Maybe they have friends in the walls of houses who tell them everything," replied the mother in a second attempt to put an end to this uncomfortable conversation.

"Are there really fairies in the walls? Then I don't want to sleep alone. I'm scared, Mum."

"I don't know, it's just a thought – I don't actually have any idea. Never mind the fairies in the walls, I just made it up. Don't be scared, honey."

"How does the fairy find out, Mum?" the girl persisted.

"You know what? It's a mystery!" the mother exclaimed, desperate to end the conversation and go eat dinner.

"Oh! Now I understand!"

Children take the existence of mystery for granted. They have a natural affinity for it because it is what keeps their desire to learn and to know alive. What is mystery? It is not merely what we do not understand. It is what we have never finished knowing. It is what has no limits. Thus, children wonder in the face of mystery because they see in it an opportunity to know the infinite; an opportunity to know that never ends. And since children are born with a sense of wonder, and wonder is the desire to learn, mystery stirs up wonder in them.

We adults, on the other hand, have no interest in this – we prefer to rationalise everything, reducing it to the measure in which we have the capacity to grasp it. Children do not have this handicap because they know that they are small, but this does not concern them. They approach mystery with humility and wonder, with a healthy uncertainty. Fanatics do not like uncertainty; they are so sure about themselves that they are incapable of seeing and learning from what is around them; they only agree with what confirms what they already think.

Children, on the other hand, learn continually, because they are at ease with uncertainty. They are comfortable with mystery because they do not impose any bias on reality, but rather approach it with humility, gratitude and openness. While some adults say that miracles do not exist, children perceive everything to be a miracle, because they do not take anything for granted. When their sense of wonder meets with mystery, they can go beyond the merely rational. Max Planck, the first winner of the Nobel Prize for Physics, said that "the progress of science consists in the discovery of a new mystery the moment one thinks that something fundamental has been solved."[1] Conversely, a person who attempts to rationalise everything to the point of excluding mystery has a reduced view of the world. Chesterton wrote, "Mysticism keeps men sane. As long as you have mystery you have health; when you destroy mystery you create morbidity . . . The madman is not the man who has lost his reason. The madman is the man who has lost everything except his reason . . . His mind moves in a perfect but narrow circle."[2]

It is therefore important that adults tread carefully in order to avoid extinguishing this quality of openness to mystery in children. This can happen if we place an exaggerated emphasis on the rational explanation of things, such as giving too detailed an explanation of the mechanism of something, in an attempt to accelerate our children's development. By giving overly detailed explanations of the mechanics of beautiful realities of life, such as sexuality, we can end up trivialising them. Children should, therefore, be gradually exposed to issues such as death, sexuality or suffering, according to the rhythm of each stage of childhood, and leaving sufficient room for mystery.

For example, it would be sad to reduce something as great as the mystery of death to something as small as an urn of ashes. The loss of a sense of mystery also leads to a loss of innocence, before our children are ready for it.

Jean Guitton, a French philosopher, said, "There are situations in which truth taught too early to a child and poorly explained in relation to other truths becomes error and becomes a cause of scandal."

Will our children fall behind if we do not explain everything to them? We are faced with a great dilemma. Either we attempt to protect our children from what does not suit them, adapting their environment to what they need, to their pace and rhythms, to their stage of development, or we accelerate their development as much as we can, because "it's inevitable, they will find out eventually". According to this position, it is useless to oppose pornographic magazines being on display in kiosks, or to initiate a debate in society on the fact that children have access to the internet through their own smartphones, that they spend hours watching television series that are not suitable for their age, and that they are made to pose sensually on magazine covers to promote items of clothing. "They will find it all out eventually." Or "we should tell them just in case – we don't want them to be the last in the class to find out." With this conformist and fatalistic argument, we give up on educating. We should teach them absolutely everything, shortening their childhood, rushing their development, scandalising them as much as we can and killing their sense of mystery – what an utterly hopeless view of education!

Protecting the gaze of our children from what is not suitable for them must not be thought of negatively, as a mere prohibition, or as a puritanical attitude, because it is not. We could even see it as a matter of prioritisation, of opportunity cost. For example, the paediatrician and researcher Dimitri Christakis states that one of the negative effects of screens is that of "the displacement effect".[3] The time that children lose in front of screens could be dedicated to other activities that are more appropriate for their development, such as quality interaction with their principal caregivers, creative play,[4] or reading. There are studies that confirm that children who spend more time in front of screens are less likely to read than those who have little screen exposure.[5] To look for quality alternatives for them is to direct their gaze toward the most beautiful. We have to give them excellent alternatives – and these exist, because we are surrounded by beautiful things. With a little wonder, we will find them without difficulty.

16

Beauty

The awful thing is that beauty is mysterious as well as terrible. God and the devil are fighting there and the battlefield is the heart of man.

Dmitri Karamazov to his brother Alyoshaen,
Fyodor Dostoyevsky, *The Brothers Karamazov*

What is it that provokes wonder? We mentioned earlier that a child marvels at the idea that something *is*, while it could just as well *not be*. But what is it in the *being* of things that provokes wonder? Various ancient philosophers enumerated the properties that are found in a thing's essence. Among these is Beauty.[¶] We can say then that beauty is one of the characteristics of the *being* that provokes wonder in children.

But what is Beauty? Is it always related to individual taste? The Beauty to which the philosophers refer is not mere aesthetic beauty subject to whims and fancies. It is not a matter of "Botox beauty" or the "cosmetic beauty" of certain celebrities. Nor is it the passing beauty of something considered beautiful by mere virtue of its being novel. These are more fashion than beauty, because they follow established parameters that, on one hand, restrict the freedom of other options, and on the other, are not necessarily true beauty because they do not stand the test of time. Fashion-beauty is subject to personal tastes, and it is for this reason that we have sayings like "it's all a matter of taste". Fashion-beauty is deeply imbedded in our culture and at times eclipses something more profound, true, and lasting.

¶ Others include unity, truth, and goodness.

The Beauty described by the philosophers is Beauty with a capital B. It is defined by Greek philosophers as *the visible expression of the Good and the True*. It was no accident when Plato wrote that "the power of the Good has taken refuge in the nature of the Beautiful." Beauty is the knowledge of the good and the true gathered through our senses and grasped by our intellect. We may not know how to appreciate it, but this should not lead us to the conclusion that it does not objectively exist. Pythagoras said he discovered it in mathematics. Because he knew so much about this topic, he saw it; knew how to appreciate it. If we do not see beauty in maths, it is not because it does not exist, but rather because we do not yet know how to see it, to appreciate it. Our ignorance of a particular subject results in our personal taste in relation to its beauty being out of line with reality. Andrei Tarkovsky, the Soviet filmmaker whose films are regularly listed among the greatest films of all time, explains why some people are not able to see Beauty where they should see it:

> The beautiful is hidden from the eyes of those who are not searching for the truth, for whom it is contra-indicated. But the profound lack of spirituality of those people who see art and condemn it, the fact that they are neither willing nor ready to consider the meaning and aim of their existence in any higher sense, is often masked by the vulgarly simplistic cry, "I don't like it!", "It's boring!" It is not a point that one can argue; but is like the utterance of a man born blind who is being told about a rainbow. He simply remains deaf to the pain undergone by the artist in order to share with others the truth he has reached.

Another example of the type of Beauty that falls within our scope would be, for instance, the life of Mother Teresa of Calcutta. Perhaps the Beauty of Mother Teresa does not fit with the common, more vulgar conception of aesthetic beauty, but we can all appreciate the beauty in her, nonetheless. Elisabeth Kübler-Ross explains:

> The most beautiful people we have known are those who have known defeat, known suffering, known struggle, known loss,

and have found their way out of the depths. These persons have an appreciation, a sensitivity, and an understanding of life that fills them with compassion, gentleness, and a deep loving concern. Beautiful people do not just happen.[1]

Beauty is found in the loving and consoling embrace of a parent, in a carefree or joyful smile, in the kindness of a sibling, in the birth of a child, in the splendour of nature. Beauty arouses a profound joy within oneself, not simply a passing feeling of attraction, fascination or satisfaction. Spanish philosopher José Ortega y Gasset writes that "beauty that attracts rarely coincides with beauty that enamours." We must not confuse fascination with wonder.

What is Beauty for a child? If Beauty is the expression of goodness and truth, the Beautiful for children would be anything that is truly good for them because it respects their true nature: their interior order, their pace and rhythms, their innocence, their innate desire for learning, etc. What children need – what is good and true for them – naturally reaches them through Beauty. The love and comfort of a child's mother are manifested in her smile, her affectionate gaze. The rhythm that suits young children arises from the delight-filled observation of nature. Discovering colours through the Beauty of the flowers in a meadow. Discovering silence through the intermittent sound of wind rustling in the leaves of a forest. It is important that children experience this through everyday things, in their true form – through the real, rather than the virtual world. For instance, it is rather curious that there is no time in school to learn how to tie shoes – even the best schools prefer that children use Velcro – yet there is enough time for structured activities designed to develop the manual dexterity of children's fingers. There is nothing like the reality of living day to day for learning new things. If we escape from our day-to-day reality to learn about it, learning ceases to be meaningful! We might ask ourselves if it is necessary to represent to children the reality of the world – the farmers' market, animals, nature, the vegetable garden – by means of flashcards, stories or films that depict, for instance, pink pigs and Bugs Bunny rabbits. A teacher of young children recounted the following anecdote to me:

One day, I asked the children to make a picture of a rabbit. They all came up with a sort of Bugs Bunny, with pink ears. There was one boy who painted a "real rabbit". With fur. Lots of fur. All the other kids laughed at his rabbit, saying it was "ugly". Isn't it strange that we sometimes see what is real as ugly, and what is artificial as beautiful?

Many children are educated in an artificial, sterile environment. They learn through instructional material and various learning props – screens, flashcards, etc. – that are a substitute for reality. Children need someone who loves them in order to orient themselves in the world, as we have mentioned earlier. To replace a loved one with a screen at such an early age dehumanises learning. Studies confirm this: young children do not learn from screens, but rather from sensory experiences and human interactions. This is not to say that modern technology is always intrinsically harmful – it isn't. We are thinking on another level, beyond the simplistic question of whether it is "good or bad". We must ask ourselves if it is truly necessary that small children begin to learn by means of new technologies. There are children who have seen a rabbit on a tablet, but have never touched one, smelt one . . . is it wise to open up an artificial world to our children before they are introduced to the real world? We must rediscover the value of a hike in the woods, a walk along the street, a visit to the farmers' market, of finding the patience to let children tie their own shoes . . . For those children who have only seen rabbits on a screen, real rabbits do not exist. Is there not a risk that reality will be overshadowed in their lives by the virtual world?

Once the importance of Beauty is understood, one must not fall into the paradigm of overstimulation with it. There are people who understand the importance of Beauty, but who transmit it to their children with an exaggerated sense of urgency, overstimulating them. At every opportunity, they shoehorn in classical music, frenzied visits to museums to learn the names of the artworks, images repeated without context, landscapes and colours flashing across screens. Everything has its proper place and must be adapted according to a child's age. Above all, the experience should take place in the real, rather than the digital world, and be relevant to the child's daily life. It is better that children spend two hours investigating a fallen leaf in their backyard than sitting in front of a screen learning about every type of tree found in the forests of Puerto Rico.

We can teach children a series of concepts, names of things, filling them with information as if they were little computers, but if we do not ensure that the reception of this knowledge is acquired through sensory experiences and is preceded by wonder, not only will the learning not last over time, but it will be meaningless. In learning that takes place without wonder, children do not have genuine respect for the familiar; they are only interested by novelty. A sense of wonder is what makes one contemplate reality with humility, gratitude, respect, a sense of mystery, and admiration. This attitude will logically affect the way children think of and respect those who act as intermediaries between them and the miracle of reality, as much in a family setting as in an educational one. This effect can explain many of the problems that we currently encounter in our homes and our classrooms and which we wrongly believe we are able to resolve with methods that allow for mechanistic indicators such as authoritarianism or permissiveness.

The wonder of a child for the Beauty of what surrounds him or her is something more natural than we might think. There is no need to stimulate children in order for them to see Beauty – they can appreciate it on their own. Children, as well as child-like adults, naturally wonder at the irresistibility of Beauty. We need only ensure that their environment be rich in Beauty, and filter out mediocrity and vulgarity, so that, as much as possible, these do not feature in their daily lives.

Beauty is never imposed, because the innocent gaze of a child perceives it without effort, or with an effort that is unnoticeable compared to the joy that Beauty provokes. We only have to let it come within their reach, as Montessori did with her young students:

> What's more, the beauty of the environment and of all the little things it contains invites the child to act, to multiply his efforts because everything ought to attract him: the colourful dusting cloths adorned with ribbons, the brooms decorated with drawings, the little toothbrushes – they are amusing

– the bars of soap, round and rectangular, pink and green. It all seems to call to the child and tell him, "Come; touch me; pick me up; clean this gleaming table with the cloth decked out for a party; take the broom that is so finely adorned and clean the floor with it; come also, adorable little hands, and immerse yourselves in water and soap."

And so it is beauty that stimulates children, responding each day to the individual dispositions that arise in their soul.[2]

Aristotle said something similar when he stated that before the habits of virtues are completely formed, certain natural inclinations pre-exist in us, which are the beginnings of the virtues, a potential for them. Children are more predisposed to the good than we are because their intentions are honest and innocent. For this reason, the mechanistic and behaviourist approach, which consists in *instilling* habits in children through the imposition of a mechanical repetition of certain actions, does not respect children's true nature. It is important to set certain limits for children, but we must educate them, keeping their powerful predisposition to virtue in mind. When children find themselves surrounded by Beauty as an expression of goodness, it is easier for them to develop habits that tend toward what is good for them and for others. Beauty is present in kindness, gentleness, compassion, understanding and gratitude. If children are surrounded by it, they will naturally assimilate it because it gives intelligent purpose to their lives. Beauty has a greater power than we suspect, and that we squander in education and in life in general.

When I think of the power of Beauty, I think of the garden full of lettuce and tomatoes in the middle of a schoolyard that children are so careful not to trample. They respect that space almost as if it were sacred. They play around it, but carefully. When I think of the power of Beauty, I also think of the following scene. For a variety of reasons, we go to a retirement home near to our home from time to time. This residence is very simple; almost austere. But there is something – it is difficult to explain what it is – that makes it Beautiful. It is located in the middle of nature, surrounded by fields of wheat and forests. It is filled with peace, serenity and smiles. The staff who work there are friendly and courteous. The elderly people who live there walk around the residence dressed plainly, but with dignity. On Sunday, the men wear suits and ties, while the women wear high heels and jewellery. They do not go to big parties, nor do they receive distinguished guests. But it is these small details that make living together pleasant for them. Very elderly couples can be seen holding hands, speaking in silence. Not long ago, I was told that the government had sent inspectors to this retirement home because people were not dying, and consequently the waiting list had not ceased to grow. I then recalled something that Dostoyevsky had said: "Man can live without science, he can live without bread, but without beauty he could no longer live, because there would no longer be anything to do in this world."

The thirst for Beauty – which is part of our search for meaning – is imbedded in our nature. However, children, or anyone who still has a child's sense of wonder, can perceive it with greater ease. Franz Kafka is reported to have said, "Youth is happy, because it has the ability to see beauty. When this ability is lost, wretched old age begins, decay, unhappiness." To which Gustav Janouch replied, "So age excludes the possibility of happiness?" Kafka responded, "No, happiness excludes age," adding, "Anyone who keeps the ability to see beauty never grows old."[3]

One of the obstacles that prevent children from seeing Beauty these days is a lack of sensitivity. We said earlier that overstimulation saturates the senses and hinders children from being able to appreciate or "sense" the aesthetic dimension of life. Overstimulation supplants wonder and prevents children from being able to perceive the Beauty of their surroundings.

17

Sensitivity

There is no such thing on earth as an uninteresting subject; the only thing that can exist is an uninterested person.

G. K. Chesterton

No art requires a longer apprenticeship than learning to see.

Jules de Goncourt

Sensory experiences allow young children not only to understand the world, but also to understand themselves within it. Everything that children touch, smell, taste, hear, and see – the real experiences they feel and the interpersonal relationships they have – leaves an impression in their mind and in their soul, through the construction of their biographical memory that develops into part of their sense of identity, through which they begin to be self-aware from about two years of age.

Sensitivity could be defined as the capacity both to perceive reality through the senses and to be in tune with its Beauty. In the same way that a person must tune into certain wavelengths in order to capture the signals of a radio station, the process of tuning a child into Beauty is achieved through sensitivity. It is a sort of focused attention or empathy with reality that allows children to sense the Beauty around them. Perhaps the reason that children have a greater ability to perceive Beauty is that their connection with the world is still deeply sensory. Sensitivity allows them to enjoy the little things, as insignificant as they may be.

One obstacle to sensitivity could be an impairment of the senses, which would impede a child from perceiving the essence of a thing. This impairment could be biological – some difficulty hearing or seeing, for instance, would restrict a child's ability to perceive Beauty through that particular sense – or could be the result of an environment that saturates the senses. Why? What is the role of sensitivity in the vicious circle of entertainment that we spoke of earlier?

When children are bombarded or strongly stimulated from without, their senses are saturated and overwhelmed by the overstimulation and their threshold for *sensing reality* reaches dramatically high levels. They will need more and more artificial stimuli in order to *feel* reality. They will become passive, bored, anxious; will be more and more dependent on their external environment in order to pay attention; and will end up losing interest in learning.

This phenomenon is considered relevant in the study of screen consumption by children. Investigation of television viewing has established a relationship between young children watching television and attentional problems later in life. Specifically, for each hour per day that children under the age of three watch television, they have a 9% greater likelihood of suffering attention deficit by the age of seven. According to the overstimulation hypothesis, "the surreal pacing and sequencing of some shows might tax the brain or parts of it, leading to short-term (or long-term) deficits."[1] In the words of Dimitri Christakis, "prolonged exposure to this rapid image change during this critical window of brain development would precondition the mind to expect high levels of input and that would lead to inattention in later life."[2] In other words, the mind of a child becomes accustomed to a reality that does not exist in everyday life – and then, when the mind turns away from fast-paced content to experience reality, it finds it boring because it cannot see beauty in the everyday. Because they do not see beauty, overstimulated children are not attracted by anything and become distracted ("distraction" is the opposite of "attraction"), and consequently, they become dependent on fast-past content in their environment.

According to a study,[3] the consumption of violent video games reduces recognition of the emotion of happiness in faces. When teenagers become accustomed to violence, their capacity to sense drops, the threshold of sensing another person's emotions increases, and so they have less empathy because they are not able to "feel with the other", leaving them to require artificial stimuli in order to connect.

Similar conclusions were reached in a study on media multitasking, carried out by Stanford's Communication between Humans and Interactive Media Lab.[4] Those who often work in "multitasking mode" produce worse results than those who do not. When our external environment saturates our senses, wonder is deadened and we cease to actively pay attention. We become passive and external stimuli *consume* our attention instead of us, ourselves, focusing our attention within our environment. This is the reason why more is not necessarily better, and learning is not exclusively dependent on one's environment, but rather on our inner ability to focus on one thought at a time and to recognise what makes sense and what does not.

As explained in the author's *Frontiers in Human Neuroscience* article,[5] what could be happening is that media multitaskers, players of violent video games, and those who consume fast-paced content at an early age, have, like any other human being, a great thirst for Beauty and meaning, but the stimuli that reach them from a multitude of sources provoke a saturation of the senses, a reduction of sensitivity, and an overall narrowed capacity that leaves them searching in the dark. Since their thirst for Beauty is not easily satisfied, they enter into a cycle of compulsive habits of consumption that causes them to *sense* less and less. This searching, oriented to information, images and so on, is a search for Beauty, for meaning – the pursuit of which, in itself, gives life purpose. But when Beauty is unattainable, it causes pain. When we compulsively seek Beauty and we do not find it, we become frustrated and unhappy. We become candidates for external motivation. In any event, what Leonardo da Vinci prophesied takes place:

> It is ordained that to the ambitious, who derive no satisfaction from the gifts of life and the beauty of the world, life shall be a cause of suffering, and they shall possess neither the profit nor the beauty of the world.

The human brain is made to learn through exposure to real-world experiences. We could say that learning happens when wonder meets with reality. But when sensitivity diminishes and the threshold of sensing increases, we need artificial stimuli to compensate for our hampered sensitivity. Young children learn through sensory contact with a slow reality, not through abstract explanations or by means of a bombardment with "perfectly designed" external stimuli. In order to preserve their sensitivity, we must let them sense. Insensitivity leads to chaos in a child's mind. John Senior explains:

> The restoration of reason presupposes the restoration of love, and we can only love what we know because we have first touched, tasted, smelled, heard and seen. From that encounter with exterior reality, interior responses naturally arise, movements motivating, urging, releasing energies, infinitely greater than atoms, of intelligence and will. Without these motives, thought and action are aimless, sometimes random, more frequently mechanical, having an order but a tyrannical order, that is, an order imposed from without.[6]

Touching damp soil or biting into and smelling a fruit leaves children with an impression that no technology can equal. It is important that they have quiet spaces in order to be able to reflect on, appreciate and relish the Beauty that surrounds them, in order to be able to develop sensitivity to the Beautiful, through aesthetic experiences that are not only found in music and art, but can also be found in kindness, or nature, for instance. Educating through sensitivity consists in surrounding children with what suits their nature – everything that respects their pace and rhythms, their innocence, etc. – and protecting their gaze from what is not suitable for them. Goodness and truth reach children through Beauty, and children grasp them through sensitivity and wonder. When this process takes place without obstacles, children truly internalise virtue and learning.

We could summarise the above using the following formulas:

**Child + Wonder + Sensitivity + Beauty + Truth =
Internalised learning**

Child + Wonder + Sensitivity + Beauty + Goodness = Inclination to virtue

Beauty helps truth and goodness penetrate us with an effort that is pleasurable – in a natural way without the need for *a priori* motivation and without falling into voluntarism. A Polish poet, Cyprian Norwid, said that "[the role of] beauty is to enthuse us to work". In Beauty, there is no tension between what one *must* and what one *wants* to do, because Beauty is where they converge.

18

Ugliness

Be yourself, be unique, be a monster!

Slogan for Monster High dolls, marketed for children

What is ugliness? Ugliness does not exist *per se*. Ugliness is the absence of Beauty. "Beauty can be found in all existing beings,"[1] said Thomas Aquinas. This means that the absence of Beauty can never be complete in anything. If something were not at least "a little bit Beautiful", then it would not exist. In other words, nothing is one hundred per cent ugly. By the very fact of *being*, it has in itself something Beautiful. This is why there is sometimes an argument over whether something is Beautiful or not, whether it suits our children's nature. This can happen when there are multiple families around the same television set on Sunday afternoon and they cannot agree about which show the children should watch. It can happen when we see what sort of gifts parents at times purchase for a birthday party: is a gothic doll with vampire teeth appropriately Beautiful for a three-year-old girl? We know that there is always Beauty in everything, but who knows if it is 10%, 20%, or 80% Beautiful? It is not as if we can know an exact percentage, because there is no such thing as a "Beauty-meter", though at times we can more easily see when there is very little. Naturally, if we, ourselves, have the sensitivity to perceive Beauty in everything that surrounds us, we will know this intuitively. So, although there is no tool that allows us to know exactly how much Beauty there is in something, it is possible to have varying levels of attunement to its presence. Insensibility makes one fall into a general attitude of blindness before Beauty, whereas sensitivity allows wonder to work more naturally, so that we tune into reality through its Beauty. This is not to say that Beauty exists only for, and belongs exclusively to, a group of special people; Beauty is everywhere and is offered to everyone, but only those with humility and sensitivity can enjoy it fully. Alejandro Jodorowsky said:

> Miracles are like stones: they are everywhere, offering up their beauty, but hardly anyone values them. We live in a reality where prodigies abound, but are seen only by those who have developed their perception of them. Without this sensitivity everything becomes banal, marvellous events are called chance, and one progresses through life without possessing the key that is gratitude. When anything extraordinary happens, it is seen as a natural phenomenon, from which we can, like parasites, profit without giving anything in exchange.[2]

In order to respect our child's wonder, we ourselves must have at least a minimal sense of gratitude, wonder and sensitivity to Beauty. Not only because children look through our eyes, but also because they will grow up in the environment that we have prepared for them. Only a sensitive caregiver knows best how to design an environment that respects the child's natural disposition.

If ugliness is the absence of Beauty, we can say that something that contains little Beauty is empty, or *banal*. Banality is that which lacks importance, originality or content. Once the wonder and sensitivity we need to enjoy beauty or aesthetic experiences are lost, the banality of emptiness springs forth, and we lose contact with the fullness of reality.

This brings us to a fundamental question: Why put children in contact with something empty, banal, vulgar and devoid of Beauty, when we could instead surround them with so much that is Beautiful? We said earlier that what is Beautiful respects children's true nature; therefore protecting their gaze from ugliness is of paramount importance. Something that does not respect their true nature – their real needs, their pace and rhythms, their interior order, etc. – can cause harm – sometimes to a great extent, such as with pornography or violence. Many children now have a lack of "vitamin B" (Beauty) in their surroundings. If we were to analyse the vast majority of television content available to children, including those programmes supposedly meant specifically for them, few would pass the Beauty test. Very few. Violent cartoons, mean-spirited dialogue, frenzied pacing, sexual insinuations, demeaning attitudes, lack of delicacy ... To surround our children with Beauty is to seek nothing less than excellence for them, accustoming them to live with a higher set of standards.

Beauty with a capital B is currently eclipsed by two trends.

First, that of **objectification**. In modern times our children are often saturated by models that promote a false, cosmetic beauty. By arousing a desire for possession and instant gratification, these models harm our children, because they convert them, specially our daughters, into objects. Furthermore, as Hermann Hesse says, "Beauty does not make the one who possesses it happy, but rather the one who loves and admires it."

Unfortunately, these models of objectification are found everywhere: in advertisements, on magazine covers and posters on the street, in merchandise – backpacks, pencil cases, umbrellas, etc. – and even in children's films, so that these become our children's best friends. From the kiss "on the lips" in *The Princess and the Frog*, where the frog makes no effort to hide his sexual attraction to Princess Tiana, to the curvy and sensual Ariel in *The Little Mermaid*, who wears seashells to cover her voluptuous breasts, these models have very little to do with our children's inner life, and contribute to over-sexualising them.

Another trend that challenges true Beauty is **the cult of ugliness**. The cult of ugliness is a form of rebellion against Beauty, according to which Beauty is a deception that must be unmasked and destroyed. According to this view, Beauty does not exist in everything; rather, Beauty is understood as a lie. The cult of ugliness acts like a pyromaniac who takes pleasure in destroying the beauty of a forest, thinking they are rendering a service to humanity. It sees lies in virtue and sincerity in vice. Systematic suspicion of all that is good and Beautiful is also a consequence of a lack of wonder. Cynicism, suspicion and universal disdain are the consequences of the loss of a capacity for admiration.

"The men where you live," said the little prince, "cultivate five thousand roses in the same garden – and they do not find in it what they are looking for."

"They do not find it," I replied.

"And yet what they are looking for could be found in one single rose, or in a little water."

"Yes, that is true," I said.

And the little prince added:

"But the eyes are blind . . ."[3]

Without Beauty, wonder works in the dark; it has nothing to take hold of. And without wonder, Beauty cannot be seen; it is as if the eye of the soul were damaged.

In recent years, the cult of ugliness has reached our children in a variety of ways, in the forms of toys, books, movies and video games. Fighting or war games contain gratuitous violence, a horrifying atmosphere, dismal figures, aggressive styling and dark designs. The success of toys like the famous gothic Monster High dolls, launched in 2010 in coffin-shaped cases and inspired by zombies and vampires, demonstrate how ugliness seeks to become a child's best friend. The question that many parents ask is, "Why are some children and teenagers attracted to ugliness?" Why this cult of ugliness that we have just described? We have already explained that it is a consequence of the loss of wonder, so everything that does not respect our children's nature is capable of contributing to this cult. Furthermore, if we pay attention, we see that many *ugly* things that are commercialised appeal to children's addiction to overstimulation. The vast majority of these dismal, violent, dark toys are accompanied by television content and extremely fast-paced video games. Children like Alex find relief in them from their addiction to stimulation.

Additionally, all the successful books, movies, television series and toys in which we see ugliness are those that involve an undercurrent of mystery. They appeal to the attraction children feel toward mystery that we explained earlier: to magic, the powers of nature, vampires, etc. It seems that the toy industry knows our children well . . .

and it knows how to win them over. An aura of mystery draws children in and facilitates the entry of the toy into their inner life. However, it is an empty, ordinary and dismal mystery. It is far from being a mystery that fills a child's life with meaning.

Children must be surrounded by Beauty in order to cure them of their lack of "vitamin B". To educate is to give opportunities for Beauty. We must seek excellence for our children and widen the horizons of their minds with what is Beautiful. Without Beauty these horizons diminish. Let us therefore not ask ourselves if the things that surround our children are 10% or 20% Beautiful, which is what we do when we justify them with, "Well, it doesn't hurt anybody." Are these things lacking in Beauty? Then, in the best of cases, they are a waste of time for our children, and in the worst, they harm them because they do not respect their true nature, their needs, their pace and rhythms, their interior order. For our children, only a great deal of Beauty will do! As Dostoyevsky said, "Beauty will save us!"

19

The role of culture

Talk to your daughter before the beauty industry does.

Dove

It is difficult to displace something that has entered into the heart of a child of zero to four years of age. It is not impossible, but it not easy either. Often, we underestimate the key role played by culture and the environment in the predisposition our children have toward a variety of positive values. It would be unreasonable to say that the environment and culture have a neutral effect on them. In education, there is nothing that is neutral.

What is culture? Culture is the expression of a way of thinking and feeling. It is transmitted through books, toys, images, words, music, the way people dress and talk, television, movies, and through the experience of each person who is in contact with our children – their classmates; their babysitter, if they have one; the bus driver, if they take the bus to school; the person who greets them at school. "It takes a village to raise a child," says the famous African proverb. Everything that enters through the senses of little children – that is, the culture and the environment – shapes their sense of identity. They do not yet have a filter: the capacity of discernment; the emotional and intellectual maturity that allows them to filter, organise, select and understand all the information they are given, based on criteria that they themselves have made their own. While they develop these criteria, the role of the educator, beginning with parents, consists in understanding to what extent a child is prepared to receive what information or observe what behaviours, and to act as an external filter, protecting the child from whatever poses a threat to his or her development at a given time.

If we want positive values to take shape in our children's sense of identity, we have to ensure that these values can be found in an obvious or subtle way in each one of the cultural elements – play, movies, people, stories, etc. – that surround our children. If these positive values that we are trying to transmit to our children are not absorbed and reflected by these cultural elements, it will be difficult for our children to assume them as their own. If those values are not part of what children perceive from their environment, it does not matter how much effort is put into *teaching* or *inculcating* them, they will permeate children's lives like a spot of oil on water.

When culture is emptied of Beauty and cedes its place to the cult of ugliness, to banality or vulgarity, positive values are perceived as a lie, or as something ridiculous, without importance, or kitschy. Children then suffer from an attitude of frivolity and insensitivity that prevents them from appreciating Beauty.

For this reason, it is important that we filter what reaches children, shaping a culture for them that adapts itself to their needs, promoting content that corresponds to the natural laws of children. If all parents did this, our streets, the television programming for certain time slots, and so forth, would be transformed into spaces free of pornography and of depressing and violent images or language. We would have a society better prepared to accept children for who they are and to provide the education that they need accordingly. All in all, we would have a society more favourable for a reawakening of wonder.

Part III

Conclusion

20

A brick wall or a beautiful mosaic

No one has yet realized the wealth of sympathy, the kindness and generosity hidden in the soul of a child. The effort of every true education should be to unlock that treasure.

Emma Goldman

Without wonder, men and women would lapse into deadening routine and little by little would become incapable of a life which is genuinely personal.

John Paul II, *Fides et Ratio*

Now, the question that might come to mind is: What is the difference between stimulation and overstimulation? If we think it over, we realise that this is in fact the wrong question, since the response is found in the nature of children themselves – in what they need at a given time – not in a cold analysis of pedagogical materials, guidelines, educational methods or a form of care foreign to them. Stimulation, *if it is not necessary from the point of view of the child's real necessities*, is excessive, and is thus an overstimulation. The person who best knows what a child needs (which is not always the same as what the child might ask for) is the caregiver who has a good quality – secure – relationship with him or her. In fact, studies tell us that what truly makes the difference in the healthy development of children is the quality of the relationship between them and their caregivers and that this quality depends on the *sensitivity* of those individuals. How well a child's development goes depends on the measure of knowledge the caregiver has of the child, their *sensitivity* to intuit what the child needs at a given time, and the *responsiveness* to promptly address these needs.

Invention, discovery, discipline and learning are compatible, Aquinas tells us, and they meet in what we have described as guided discovery. According to neuroscience, this should occur in an average environment with a minimal amount of sensory stimulation. Otherwise, in the best of cases overstimulation would be a waste of time, and in the worst, an addition that could provoke chaos in the child's mind, as well as undesired behaviours, as we have seen earlier.

We might also wonder about the value of certain educational methods. If it is indeed true that there are methods that are in themselves objectively mechanistic, or others that, on the contrary, are respectful of children's nature, it is necessary to go further and ascertain what circumstances of their use can attenuate or exaggerate the impact of their effects. The method is not everything and must not be decontextualised from the child, from the paradigm of the educator (the way he or she understands childhood), from the management style of the school, or from the child's macro- (society) and micro- (school and home) environments. Each case must be studied carefully, without falling into a search for a standardised recipe.

In fact, we are increasingly victims of the industry of educational advice and of the pre-packaged formula that resolves the *how* – the mechanistic approach – passing over the *why* and *what for* of education. Parents should never seek "the easy formula". First, because we should not believe those who imply that educating is easy; second because no standard formula exists for all the variety of circumstances of life of each one of our children; and finally because we have to escape the mechanistic models that distract us and distance us from the true *raison d'être* in education: the person. Each family is its own universe; each child is its own universe. In order to respond to doubts or questions posed by parents and educators, it is necessary to know the child (his or her age, circumstances and family situation), the context of the method (the educator's approach to education, the frequency with which a method is applied, the means through which it is transmitted, the objective, etc.), the family situation (whether the child has a secure attachment or not, for example), etc.

For instance, there is a big difference between children watching a fast-paced as opposed to a slow-paced cartoon. With their parents or without their parents. At the age of one or at the age of six. At nine in the morning, at five o'clock, or just before they go to bed. In a movie theatre or in front of a tiny screen. With violence or without violence. Because their parents are convinced that they will learn English this way – infants do not learn languages from movies – or because it is a way we are trying to survive the afternoon while we are giving our youngest children a bath. It is very different to read a story to 500 children in an auditorium with a microphone in front of a bright and flashy screen and with deafening background music, as opposed to a smaller group of children in their usual classroom. It is very different if the intermediary between the story and the children is a digital screen as opposed to the teacher who spends every day with them. It makes a difference if the story is adapted to the age of the children or not. For example, it is not the same thing to want to encourage independence in children by letting them do what they feel able to do (getting dressed in the morning, putting on an apron on their own) as to push them to do something that they do not feel capable of doing, simply because "it's time to learn", because it is a milestone. In general, a sensitive educator, whether a parent or teacher, knows what children need and what they are prepared to do on their own at each stage of their development. Thus, if we want to adopt the Wonder Approach and our children go to preschool, the most important thing is to find a preschool for our children that is run by people with a great sensitivity to this approach.

Further, it is important not to reduce the discussion on the Wonder Approach to a series of techniques, advice, methods and prohibitions. The Wonder Approach is not a method. To adopt the Wonder Approach is to let our children bring their eyes up to a keyhole in a door that opens up into the real world. When our children see the keyhole from a distance, they can see only a faint ray of light. As they come closer to the door, what they see grows, until one day, with their forehead pressed against the door lock, they find themselves contemplating the Beauty of the universe. The Wonder Approach is a philosophy of life.

The Wonder Approach is not about going back in time, out of nostalgia for the past. It is true that in some way it is "the same old, same old", but it must be applied to the circumstances of the time in which we now find ourselves, and that in which we will find ourselves tomorrow. Sometimes we confuse originality with novelty. Gaudí once said that "to be original is to return to the origin." The Wonder Approach goes far beyond mere cultural and temporal features, because it is founded on the natural laws of the child; atemporal and transcending culture. To adopt the Wonder Approach is to recognise that our children have a nature that is proper to them, to which we should be sensitive and attentive. Children are the primary agents of their education. They do not need us to stimulate them from the outside in. Children discover through wonder, and it is this wonder that makes them desire knowledge, which motivates them to act and to want to learn. No, our children do not need us to transform ourselves into playroom entertainers or long for us to transform their childhood into something magical, because their childhood is already magical, in and of itself.

To educate with the Wonder Approach is to respect their pace and rhythms, their basic needs, their innocence; to avoid rushing their development. Embracing the Wonder Approach allows children to appreciate Beauty. To educate through Beauty so that they can find reasons to wonder. To cultivate their sensitivity so they can wonder at Beauty. The child, wonder, sensitivity and Beauty. Four variables that have been lost from view in our day and age and to which we must return their proper place and their importance. There is a great deal at stake for us. Far more than we can ever imagine.

To abandon wonder and surround children with things that have little Beauty is to denaturalise them, robbing them of their childhood and diminishing the horizons of their mind. It also means abandoning the possibility of them being everything that they can potentially be as teenagers and as adults. Children whose sense of wonder has been erased are set to become teenagers and then adults who are . . .

- Unmotivated like Emma, whose desire to learn has been stifled.

- Ungrateful, because they think that they have a right to everything.
- Compelled to seek new sensations because they are used to having their senses saturated.
- Blind to the Beauty of the world because their loss of a sense of mystery means that they reduce everything to something they can rationalise.
- Cynical, a state contrary to wonder, which will lead them to an attitude of universal disdain.
- Suspicious of the good and the Beautiful, substituting both with the cult of ugliness.

Such a child is and will be, as the famous song by Pink Floyd says, "another brick in the wall". A conformist child, a weary soul, disenchanted with the world that surrounds him or her. And a society formed by such people is not sustainable, because the desire for improvement and the recognition of what is good and what is beautiful without scepticism, without cynicism, without envy, without scorn, are necessary for the progress of any society.

Adolescence does have some features that seemingly stem from a lack of wonder, because this stage of life sometimes involves a questioning of what one is told, in order to decide whether "to make it my own or not". However, these characteristics are simply proper to that stage of life. So adolescence is not a phase that we can pretend to "quick-fix" with the Wonder Approach. With wonder we give teenagers more opportunities.

However, children whose wonder we have allowed to blossom will be set to reach adolescence as people who . . .

- Will be grateful, because they will not take everything for granted.
- Will ponder things in their hearts and be introspective, because they have inner life.
- Will know how to recognise what is superior, without envy or stinginess.
- Will be able to appreciate Beauty, because their gaze

will not be superficial, but will penetrate beyond mere appearances.

- Will be patient, because they will be used to waiting before receiving.
- Will not reduce life to a series of experiences or a succession of facts without transcendence, but will consider it as an adventure of seeking goodness, of discovering reality, of appreciating Beauty, and of selecting everything according to its intrinsic value.
- Will be calm and tranquil, because their senses will not have been dulled.
- Will live everyday life meaningfully, with intelligent purpose, so that they will not spend their lives seeking new sensations.
- Will act out of conviction, because they will not find their source of motivation in other people or circumstances.
- Will be compassionate towards others, because they will know how to go out of themselves and have the sensitivity to perceive the needs of others.
- Will be reflective and open to mystery, because they will not reduce reality to what can be understood; this will arouse in them an infinite thirst for knowledge and discovery, and will open the way to true progress in their lives and in society.

Now, I appeal to your sense of wonder: imagine for a moment what a beautiful mosaic humanity would form if every human being embodied these traits.

21

The invisible citizen

*Every child comes with the message that God is not yet
discouraged of man.*

Rabindranath Tagore

*Children are the future not because they will one day be
adults but because humanity is becoming more and more a
child, because childhood is the image of the future.*

Milan Kundera

If we wish to recreate a culture of wonder, it is necessary to reverse
many of the paradigms that have guided us in children's education:
converting children into tailor-made products, into little, manageable
adults, to the point that this seems to have become the *raison d'être* of
children's education. Children are children! They are not "unfinished"
or "imperfect" adults. It seems that we are searching for the perfect
snapshot of our children, but there is no perfect snapshot; they are
on life's journey, just as we are. Trees, for example, begin as little
shoots, sending forth little branches, then delicate leaves. They grow
according to the rhythm of their own nature. The Wonder Approach
is not overprotection of children, pruning them like a bonsai to avoid
their growth. Rather, it is letting them grow at their own pace and
rhythm, giving them what they need and protecting them from whatever is not suitable for them. People are born babies, then they are
children, then they are adults, and then they enter old age. There is
no such thing as a "finished human being". We are all born with a
certain order, a rhythm that corresponds and that is proper to each of

our stages of development. To the extent that children are not able to harmonise this interior order with their environment, because it is not tailored to their real needs, it creates a tension in them; a lack of unity, which provokes that "cry of nature" that Montessori described so well and that could well be the root of many of the disorders that we now increasingly observe in children. As has been said many times, "God always forgives, man sometimes forgives, but nature never forgives."

Montessori states that children, without being conscious of it, play a key role in society and in adult life, and explains how much our world would change if we understood the significance of this affirmation. The following quote dates to the year 1965, but it has a curious relevance:

> There are some . . . who think that the child's only value for humanity lies in the fact that he will someday be an adult. . . The child is a human entity having importance in himself; he is not just a transition on the way to adulthood. We ought not to consider the child and the adult merely as successive phases in the individual's life. *We ought rather to look upon them as two different forms of human life, going on at the same time, and exerting upon one another a reciprocal influence.* The child and the adult are in fact two different and separate parts of humanity which should interpenetrate and work together in the harmony of mutual aid . . .

> When it comes to helping the child in his psychic and spiritual needs we often see an almost contrary attitude in the parents. Without their being properly aware of it, the struggle with the child now begins. They consider him too much of a possession and treat him as such. Now they consider that the child should be what *they* wish him to be. Children ought to find pleasure in and be interested in what their parents choose to impose on them. They should be pleased with an environment created exclusively to suit the interests and practical comfort of adults . . . If educators . . . allowed themselves to be guided by his true needs, the child's life would be more profoundly influenced, and for a longer time, by the

special mentality and the special environment required by these needs.

Then civilization would not develop exclusively from the point of view of what is convenient and useful for adult life. Today progress is sought for, too much and too exclusively, through adult qualities. Thus civilization is based on the triumph of force, on violent conquest, on adaptation, on the struggle for existence and the survival of the conquerors. The sad consequences of this development show themselves in the religious-moral field, in social economics and in international politics. All these things are a living proof that in the construction of society something – some essential element – has been missing; that the characteristics of the child have had too little influence, because he and the adult have been too far apart. The child has almost disappeared from the thoughts of the adult world, and the adults live too much as though there were no children who have the right to influence them . . .

In certain sections of society the child has come to be regarded merely as a possession, to be acquired or not according to one's own inclinations. One or two children – yes, that is pleasant – so that one does not feel too lonely, and can amuse oneself with these doll-playthings! . . . If we were to change the center of civilization from the adult to the child a more noble form of civilization would arise.[1]

The time has come to change society so that it is better tailored to the needs of children. A civilisation that is exclusively founded on adult values is destined to fail. We must return to including not only children in society, but also all the values that represent them, beginning with wonder. Children remind us of the values of peace, solidarity, transparency, gentleness, optimism, the protection of innocence, empathy, compassion, the dignity of human life, joy, gratitude, humility, simplicity, and friendship.

It is never too late to recover a lost sense of wonder. In fact, discovering wonder as something good and desirable and desiring to recover it is the best starting point, because this is, in itself, a manifestation of wonder. Chesterton once wrote that "the world will never starve for want of wonders; but only for want of wonder." The Wonder Approach is an attempt to prove Chesterton's prophecy wrong, so that, in the midst of a world filled with distractions, our children can wonder again at the irresistible beauty that surrounds them.

Notes

Introduction

1   Postman, N. (2006). *Amusing ourselves to death: Public discourse in the age of show business*. Penguin.

2   U.S. Department of Health and Human Services. (1999). *Mental health: A report of the surgeon general*. Rockville, MD: Administration National Institute of Mental Health, Department of Health and Human Services, Substance Abuse and Mental Health Services.

3   Ra, C. K., Cho, J., Stone, M. D., De La Cerda, J., Goldenson, N. I., Moroney, E., . . . Leventhal, A. M. (2018). Association of Digital Media Use With Subsequent Symptoms of Attention-Deficit/Hyperactivity Disorder Among Adolescents. JAMA, *320*(3), 255.

4   Mayo Clinic. (2017). Attention-deficit/hyperactivity disorder (ADHD) in children - Symptoms and causes -. Retrieved 8 November, 2018, from https://www.mayoclinic.org/diseases-conditions/adhd/symptoms-causes/syc-20350889

5   Aquinas, T. *Summa Theologiae*, Question 32, Article 8 (1a2ae 32.8). Online edition. www.newadvent.org/summa.

6   Berger, J., & Milkman, K. (2011). What makes online content viral? *Journal of Marketing Research*.

7   Aristotle. (2014). *Metaphysics*. (W. D. Ross, Trans.). Australia: eBooks@Adelaide, The University of Adelaide; Plato. (2014). *Theaetetus*. (B. Jowett, Trans.). Australia: eBooks@Adelaide, The University of Adelaide.

8   Watson, J. B. (1930). *Behaviorism*. Chicago, IL: University of Chicago Press.

9   Huxley, T. H., & Youmans, W. J. (1868). *The elements of physiology and hygiene: A text-book for educational institutions*. New York, NY: Appleton & Co.

Chapter One

1   Chesterton, G. K. (2014). *The G. K. Chesterton Collection.* (50 books). London: Catholic Way Publishing.

Chapter Two

1   Montessori, M. (1936). *The secret of childhood.* London: Ballantine Books.
2   U.S. Department of Health and Human Services. (2011). *Head Start impact study.*
3   Howard-Jones, P. (2007). Neuroscience and education: Issues and opportunities, commentary by the Teacher and Learning Research Programme. London: Economic and Social Research Council, TLRP.
4   Ibid.
5   Christakis, D. A., Ramirez, J. S. B., & Ramirez, J. M. (2012). Overstimulation of newborn mice leads to behavioural differences and deficits in cognitive performance. *Scientific Reports, 2,* 246.
6   Among others, Goswami, U. (2006). Neuroscience and education: From research to practice. *Nature Reviews Neuroscience, 7,* 406–413; Dekker, S., Lee, N. C., Howard-Jones, P., & Jolles, J. (2012). Neuromyths in education: Prevalence and predictors of misconceptions among teachers. *Frontiers in Psychology, 3,* 429; Howard-Jones, P. A. (2014). Neuroscience and education: Myths and messages. *Nature Reviews Neuroscience, 15,* 817–824; Deligiannidi, K., & Howard-Jones, P. A. (2015). The neuroscience literacy of teachers in Greece. *Social and Behavioral Sciences, 174,* 3909–3915; Ferrero, M., Garaizar, P., & Vadillo, M. (2016). Neuromyths in education: Prevalence among Spanish teachers and an exploration of cross-cultural variation. *Frontiers in Human Neuroscience, 10,* 496; Pei, X., Howard-Jones, P. A., Zhang, S., Liu, X., & Jin, Y. (2015). Teachers' understanding about the brain in East China. *Social and Behavioral Sciences, 194,* 3681–3688.
7   Organization for Economic Co-operation and Development. (2002). *Understanding the brain: Towards a new learning science.* Paris, France: OECD.
8   See note 3; Hyatt, K. J. (2007). Brain Gymä building stronger

brains or wishful thinking? *Remedial and Special Education, 28*(2), 117–124. The idea of Brain Gym is founded on the patterning theory also adapted by Doman and Delacato for the treatment of brain injuries and to "accelerate learning" in healthy babies and children. The American Academy of Neurology and the American Academy of Pediatrics have issued a statement regarding the lack of scientific foundation of these claims: American Academy of Pediatrics. (1968). The Doman-Delacato treatment of neurologically handicapped children. *Neurology*, 18, 1.214–1.215; American Academy of Pediatrics. (1999). The treatment of neurologically impaired children using patterning. *Pediatrics, 104*, 1.149–1.151.

9   Garrison, M., & Christakis, D. A. (2005). *A teacher in the living room: Educational media for babies, toddlers, and preschoolers.* Menlo Park, CA: The Henry J. Kaiser Family Foundation.

10 The Henry J. Kaiser Family Foundation. (2004). *Parents, media and public policy: A Kaiser Family Foundation survey.* Menlo Park, CA.

11 Infant, preschooler DVDs. (2005). *Drug Store News, 27*(2), 38; https://www.kqed.org/mindshift/18258/explosive-growth-in-education-apps

12 Among these are: Richert, R. A., Robb, M. B., Fender, J. G., & Wartella, E. (2010). Word learning from baby videos. *Archives of Pediatrics & Adolescent Medicine, 164*(4), 432–437; Kuhl, P. K., Tsao, F. M., & Liu, H. M. (2003). Foreign-language experience in infancy: Effects of short-term exposure and social interaction on phonetic learning. *Proceedings of the National Academy of Sciences of the United States of America, 100*(15), 9096–9101.

13 Zimmerman, F. J., Christakis, D. A., & Meltzoff A. N. (2007). Associations between media viewing and language development in children under age 2 years. *The Journal of Pediatrics, 151*(4), 364; Chonchaiya, W., & Pruksananonda, C. (2008). Television viewing associates with delayed language development. *Acta Paediatrica, 97*(7), 977–982; Tomopoulos, S., Dreyer, B. P., Berkule, S., Fierman, A. H., Brockmeyer, C., & Mendelsohn, A. L. (2010). Infant media exposure and toddler development. *Archives of Pediatrics & Adolescent Medicine, 164*(12), 1105–1111.

14 Linebarger, D. L., & Walker, D. (2005). Infants' and toddlers' television viewing and language outcomes. *American Behavioral Scientist, 48*(5), 624–645.

15 Canadian Paediatric Society. (2017). Screen time and young children: Promoting health and development in a digital world. *Paediatrics & Child Health, 22*(8), 461–468.

16 See note 15; American Academy of Pediatrics. (2016). Media and young minds. *Pediatrics, 138*(5). It confirms its recommendations of 2011 and 1999 (cf. American Academy of Pediatrics. (2011). Policy statement on media use by children younger than 2 years. *Pediatrics, 128*(5), 1040–1045).

17 Siegel, J. D. (2001). Toward an interpersonal neurobiology of the developing mind: Attachment relationships, "mindsight", and neural integration. *Infant Mental Health Journal, 22*(1–2), 67–94.

18 Siegel, J. D. (1999). *Toward a biology of compassion: Relationships, the brain and the development of mindsight across the lifespan.* Document presented to John Paul II and the Pontifical Council for the Family, Vatican City, December 1999.

19 Chesterton, G. K. (2004). *Orthodoxy.* MT: Kessinger Publishing.

Chapter Three

1 Christakis, D. A. (2011). The effects of fast-pace cartoons. *Pediatrics, 128*(4).

2 Goodrich, S. A., Pempek, T. A., & Calvert, S. L. (2009). Formal production features of infant and toddler DVDs. *Archives of Pediatrics & Adolescent Medicine, 163*(12), 1151–1156.

3 Swing, E. L., Gentile, D. A., Anderson, C. A., & Walsh, D. A. (2010). Television and video game exposure and the development of attention problems. *Pediatrics, 126*(2), 214–221; Barlett, C. P., Anderson, C. A., & Swing, E. L. (2009). Video game effects confirmed, suspected, and speculative: A review of the evidence. *Simulation Gaming, 40*, 377–403.

4 Christakis, D. A., Zimmerman, F. J., DiGiuseppe, D. L., & McCarty, C. A. (2004). Early television exposure and subsequent attentional problems in children. *Pediatrics, 111*(4), 708–713; Zimmerman, F. J., & Christakis, D. A. (2007). Associations between content

types of early media exposure and subsequent attentional problems. *Pediatrics, 120*(5), 986–992.

5   Christakis, D. A. (2010). Infant media viewing: First, do no harm. *Pediatric Annals, 39*(9), 578–582.

6   See Chapter 2, note 19.

7   See note 5; Christakis, D. A. (2008). The effects of infant media usage: What do we know and what should we learn? *Acta Paediatrica, 98*(1), 8–16.

8   Johnson, J., Cohen, P., Kasen, S., & Brook, J. S. (2007). Extensive television viewing and the development of attention and learning difficulties during adolescence. *Archives of Pediatrics and Adolescent Medicine, 161*(5), 480–486; Hancox, R. J., Milne, B. J., & Poulton, R. (2005). Association of television viewing during childhood with poor educational achievement. *Archives of Pediatrics and Adolescent Medicine, 159*(7), 614–618; Pagani, L. S., Fitzpatrick, C., Barnett, T. A., & Dubow, E. (2010). Prospective associations between early childhood television exposure and academic, psychosocial, and physical well-being by middle childhood. *Archives of Pediatrics and Adolescent Medicine, 164*(5), 425–431.

9   Montessori, M. (1965). *The child in the Church*. E. M. Standing (Ed.). Chantilly, France: Catechetic.

10 Calfas, J. (2017, May 11). *Do fidget spinners really help with ADHD? Nope, experts say. Money. Time*. Retrieved 16 May 2017.

Chapter Six

1   Aquinas, T. (1953). *Questiones disputatae de veritate*. Question 11, article 1 (J. V. McGlynn, Trans.). Chicago, IL: Henry Regnery Company.

2   Ibid., article 2.

3   Ibid., article 1.

4   Guardini, R. (1997). *Las etapas de la vida: Su importancia para la ética y la pedagogía*. Biblioteca Plabra. (Our translation)

5   Aquinas, T., op. cit., article 3.

6   Barker, J. E., Semenov, A. D., Michaelson, L., Provan, L. S., Snyder, H. R., & Munakata Y. (2014). Less-structured time in children's daily lives predicts self-directed executive functioning. *Frontiers in Psychology*.

7   Ginsburg, K. R., American Academy of Pediatrics, Committee on Communications, Committee on Psychosocial Aspects of Child and Family Health. (2007). The importance of play in promoting healthy child development and maintaining strong parent-child bonds. *Pediatrics, 119*(1), 182–191.

8   Barkley, R. A. (1997). Behavioral inhibition, sustained attention, and executive functions: Constructing a unifying theory of ADHD. *Psychological Bulletin, 121*(1), 65–94.

9   Singer, J. L. (2002). Cognitive and affective implications of imaginative play in childhood. In M. Lewis (Comp.), *Child and adolescent psychiatry: A comprehensive textbook* (3rd ed., pp. 252–263). Philadelphia, PA: Lippincott Williams & Wilkins.

10   Engel, S. (2011). Children's need to know: Curiosity in schools. *Harvard Educational Review, 81*(4), 625–645.

11   Kim, K. H. (2011). The creativity crisis: The decrease in creative thinking scores on the Torrance Tests of Creative Thinking. *Creativity Research Journal, 23*(4), 285–295.

12   Csikszentmihalyi, M. (1975). *Beyond boredom and anxiety: Experiencing flow in work and play*. San Francisco, CA: Jossey-Bass.

13   Goertzel, M. G., & Goertzel, V. H. (1960). Intellectual and emotional climate in families procuring eminence. *Gifted Child Quarterly, 4*, 59–60.

Chapter Seven

1   Honoré, C. (2010). *Under pressure: Putting the child back in childhood*. Knopf Canada.

2   Aristotle. (2009). Nicomachean ethics (Bk. II, Ch. 3). In R. McKeon (Ed.), *The Basic Works of Aristotle*. New York, NY: Random House.

3   Montessori, M. (1967). *The absorbent mind*. New York, NY: Delta.

Chapter Eight

1   American Academy of Pediatrics. (n.d.) Winter Safety Tips. *1/2, Safekids*. Retrieved in July 2014.

2   Carson, R. (2011). *The sense of wonder*. Open Road Media.

3   Flowers, W. (2007, October 23). *Ceremonia investidura grado*

honoris causa universidad Andrés Bello Dr. Woodie Flowers [Dr. Woodie Flowers *honoris causa* investiture ceremony Andrés Bello University]. https://web.archive.org/web/20110929144708/http://www.unab.cl/flowers/descargas/discurso2.pdf

Chapter Nine

1 Touchette, E., Côté, S., Petit, D., Xuecheng, L., Boivin, M., Falissard, B., Montplaisir, J. Y. (2009). Short nighttime sleep-duration and hyperactivity trajectories in early childhood. *Pediatrics, 124*(5), 985–993; Bernier, A., Carlson S. M., Bordeleau, B., & Carrier, J. (2010). Relations between physiological and cognitive regulatory systems: Infant sleep regulation and subsequent executive functioning. *Child Development, 81*(6), 1739–1752; Ednick M., Cohen, A. P., McPhail, G. L., Beebe, D., Simakajornboon, N., & Amin, R. S. (2009). A review of the effects of sleep during the first year of life on cognitive, psychomotor, and temperament development. *Sleep, 1*(32), 1449–1458; Beebe, D. W. (2011). Cognitive, behavioral, and functional consequences of inadequate sleep in children and adolescents. *Pediatric Clinics of North America, 58*, 649–665; Berger R. H., Miller A. L., Seifer, R., Cares, S. R., & Lebourgeois, M. K. (2011). Acute sleep restriction effects on emotion responses in 30- to 36-month-old children. *Journal of Sleep Research.*
2 American Academy of Pediatrics. (2016). Media and young minds. *Pediatrics, 138*(5); American Academy of Pediatrics. (2016). Media use in school-aged children and adolescents. *Pediatrics, 138*(5).

Chapter Ten

1 See Chapter 6, note 6.
2 See Chapter 6, note 4.

Chapter Eleven

1 Samples, B. (1977) Mind Cycles and Learning. *Phi Delta Kappa International. 58*(9), 689.

Chapter Twelve

1   Schmitt, M. E., Pempek, T. A., Kirkorian, H. L., Lund, A. F., & Anderson, D. R. (2008). The effect of background television on the toy play behavior of very young children. *Child Development, 79*(4), 1137–1151.

2   Tanimura, M., Okuma, K., & Kyoshima, K. (2007). Television viewing, reduced parental utterance, and delayed speech development in infants and young children. *Archives of Pediatrics and Adolescent Medicine, 161*(6), 618–619; Mendelsohn, A. L., Berkule, S. B., & Tomopoulos, S. (2008). Infant television and video exposure associated with limited parent-child verbal interactions in low socioeconomic status households. *Archives of Pediatrics and Adolescent Medicine, 162*(5), 411–417; Christakis, D. A., Gilkerson, J., Richards, J. A., Zimmerman, F. J., Garrison, M. M., Xu, D. . . . Yapanel, U. (2009). Audible television and decreased adult words, infant vocalizations, and conversational turns: A population-based study. *Archives of Pediatrics and Adolescent Medicine, 162*(5), 411–417.

3   Guardini, R. (1981). La situación incompleta del hombre actual [The incomplete situation of the modern man]. In *Obras Selectas I* [Selected Works I]. Madrid, Spain: Ediciones Cristiandad.

4   Promethean. (2012). *Educación 3.0, la revista para el aula del siglo XXI* [Education 3.0, the magazine for the 21st century classroom], *6*, 28.

5   Richtel, M. (2011). A Silicon Valley school that doesn't compute. *The New York Times* (digital version).

6   Bilton, N. (2014). Steve Jobs was a Low-Tech Parent. *The New York Times* (digital version).

7   Bowles, N. (2018). Silicon Valley Nannies are Phone Police for Kids. *The New York Times* (digital version).

8   Bowles, N. (2018). The Digital Gap Between Rich and Poor Kids Is Not What We Expected. *The New York Times* (digital version).

9   Rowlands, I., Nicholas D., Williams P., Huntington, P., Fieldhouse M., Gunter B., et al. (2008). The Google generation: The information behaviour of the researcher of the future. *Art Libraries Journal, 35*(1), 18–21.

10 Kirschner, P., De Bruyckere, P. (2017). The myths of the digital native and the multitasker. *Teaching and Teacher Education*. 67, 135–142.

11 Carr, N. (2008). Is Google making us stupid? What the Internet is doing to our brains. *The Atlantic, 301*(6).

Chapter Thirteen

1 de Saint-Exupéry, A. (2000). *The Little Prince* (R. Howard, Trans.). Mariner Books.

Chapter Fourteen

1 Fulghum, R. cited in Zimmer, B. J. (2003). Reflections for Tending the Sacred Garden. *iUniverse*. 296. P.182.

2 Kirschner, P. A., Sweller, J., & Clark, R. E. (2006). Why minimal guidance during instruction does not work: An analysis of the failure of constructivist, discovery, problem-based, experiential, and inquiry-based teaching. *Journal of Educational Psychology,* 41, 75–86; Mayer, R. E. (2004). Should there be a three-strikes rule against pure discovery learning? *American Psychologist, 59,* 14–19; Bryant, J., Dorn, E., Kihn, P., Krawitz, M., Mourshed, M., & Sarakatsannis, J. (2017). *Drivers of student performance: Insights from North America*. Retrieved from McKinsey & Company website.

3 Barber, M., & Mourshed, M. (2007). *How the world's best-performing school systems came out on top*. Retrieved from McKinsey & Company website.

4 Canadian Paediatric Society. (2017). Screen time and young children: Promoting health and development in a digital world. *Paediatrics & Child Health, 22*(8), 461–468.

5 Lerner, C., & Barr, R. (2014). Screen sense: Setting the record straight; Research-based guidelines for screen use for children under 3 years old. *Zero to Three*; Klein-Radukic, S., & Zmyj, N. (2016). The relation between contingency preference and imitation in 6–8-month-old infants. *International Journal of Behavioral Development, 40*(2), 173–180; Moser, A., Zimmerman, L., Dickerson, K., Grenell, A., Barr, R., & Gerhardstein, P. (2015). They can interact, but can they

learn? Toddlers' transfer learning from touchscreens and television. *Journal of Experimental Child Psychology, 137*, 137–155; Barr, R. (2010). Transfer of learning between 2D and 3D sources during infancy: Informing theory and practice. *Developmental Review, 30*(2), 128–154.

6   Canfield Fisher, D. (1914). *Mothers and children*. New York: H. Holt and Company.

Chapter Fifteen

1   Planck, M. (1932). *Where is science going?* New York, NY: W. W. Norton & Company, Inc.

2   See Chapter 2, note 19.

3   See Chapter 3, note 5.

4   Vandewater, E. A., Bickham, D. S., & Lee, J. H. (2006). Time well spent? Relating television use to children's free-time activities. *Pediatrics, 117*(2).

5   Vandewater, E. A., Bickham, D. S., Lee, J. H., Cummings, H. M., Wartella, E. A., & Rideout, V. J. (2005). When the television is always on: Heavy television exposure and young children's development. *American Behavioral Scientist, 48*(5), 562–577.

Chapter Sixteen

1   Kübler-Ross, E. (1975). *The Final Stage of Growth*. Scribner.

2   Montessori, M. (1989). *The child in the family*. The Clio Montessori Series, vol. 8. ABC: CLIO.

3   Janouch, G. (2012). *Conversations with Kafka* (2nd ed.). New York: New Directions Publishing.

Chapter Seventeen

1   See Chapter 3, note 1.

2   TED. (2011, December 28). *TedxRainier – Dimitri Christakis – Media and children* [Video file]. Retrieved from https://www.you tube.com/watch?v=BoT7qH_uVNo

3   Kirsh, S. J., & Mounts, J. R. (2007). Violent video game play impacts facial emotion recognition. *Aggressive Behavior, 33*, 353–358.

4   Ophir, E., Nass, C., & Wagner, A. D. (2009). Cognitive control in media multitaskers. *Proceedings of the National Academy of Sciences of the United States of America, 106*(37), 15,583–15,587.

5   L'Ecuyer, C. (2014). The Wonder Approach to learning. *Frontiers in Human Neuroscience*.

6   Senior, J. (1983). *The Restoration of the Christian Culture*. San Francisco: Ignatius Press.

Chapter Eighteen

1   Aquinas, T. (1965). *The pocket Aquinas* (4th ed.). (V. J. Bourke, Trans.). New York, NY: Washington Square Press.

2   Jodorowsky, A. (2014). *The Dance of Reality: A Psychomagical Autobiography*. New York: Simon & Schuster.

3   See Chapter 13, note 1.

Chapter Twenty-one

1   See Chapter 3, note 10.

References

American Academy of Pediatrics. (n.d.) Winter Safety Tips. *1/2, Safekids*. Retrieved in July 2014.

American Academy of Pediatrics. (1968). The Doman-Delacato treatment of neurologically handicapped children. *Neurology, 18*, 1214–1215.

American Academy of Pediatrics. (1999). The treatment of neurologically impaired children using patterning. *Pediatrics, 104*, 1149–1151.

American Academy of Pediatrics. (2011). Policy statement on media use by children younger than 2 years. *Pediatrics, 128(5)*, 1040–1045.

American Academy of Pediatrics. (2016). Media and young minds. *Pediatrics, 138(5)*.

American Academy of Pediatrics. (2016). Media use in school-aged children and adolescents. *Pediatrics, 138(5)*.

Aquinas, T. (1920). *Summa Theologiae*. Ed. Kevin Knight. Online edition. www.newadvent.org/summa.

Aquinas, T. (1953). *Questiones disputatae de veritate*. (J. V. McGlynn, Trans.). Chicago, IL: Henry Regnery Company.

Aquinas, T. (1965). *The pocket Aquinas* (4th ed.). (V. J. Bourke, Trans.). New York, NY: Washington Square Press.

Barber, M., & Mourshed, M. (2007). *How the world's best-performing school systems came out on top*. Retrieved from McKinsey & Company website: https://www.mckinsey.com/~/media/mckinsey/industries/social%20sector/our%20insights/how%20the%20worlds%20best%20performing%20school%20systems%20come%20out%20on%20top/how_the_world_s_best-performing_school_systems_come_out_on_top.ashx

Barker, J. E., Semenov, A. D., Michaelson, L., Provan, L. S., Snyder, H. R., & Munakata Y. (2014). Less-structured time in children's daily lives predicts self-directed executive functioning. *Frontiers in Psychology*.

Barkley, R. A. (1997). Behavioral inhibition, sustained attention, and executive functions: Constructing a unifying theory of ADHD. *Psychological Bulletin*, 121(1), 65–94.

Barlett, C. P., Anderson, C. A., & Swing, E. L. (2009). Video game effects confirmed, suspected, and speculative: A review of the evidence. *Simulation Gaming, 40*, 377–403.

Barr, R. (2010). Transfer of learning between 2D and 3D sources during infancy: Informing theory and practice. *Developmental Review, 30(2)*, 128–154.

Beebe, D. W. (2011). Cognitive, behavioral, and functional consequences of inadequate sleep in children and adolescents. *Pediatric Clinics of North America, 58*, 649–665.

Berger, J., & Milkman, K. (2011). What makes online content viral? *Journal of Marketing Research.*

Berger, R. H., Miller, A. L., Seifer, R., Cares, S. R., & Lebourgeois, M. K. (2011). Acute sleep restriction effects on emotion responses in 30- to 36-month-old children. *Journal of Sleep Research, 21(3)*, 235–246.

Bernier, A., Carlson, S. M., Bordeleau, B., & Carrier, J. (2010). Relations between physiological and cognitive regulatory systems: Infant sleep regulation and subsequent executive functioning. *Child Development, 81(6)*, 1739–1752.

Bilton, N. (2014). Steve Jobs was a Low-Tech Parent, *The New York Times* (digital version).

Bowles, N. (2018). Silicon Valley Nannies are Phone Police for Kids. *The New York Times* (digital version).

Bowles, N. (2018). The Digital Gap Between Rich and Poor Kids Is Not What We Expected. *The New York Times* (digital version).

Bryant, J., Dorn, E., Kihn, P., Krawitz, M., Mourshed, M., & Sarakatsannis, J. (2017). *Drivers of student performance: Insights from North America*. Retrieved from McKinsey & Company website: https://www.mckinsey.com/~/media/McKinsey/Industries/Social%20Sector/Our%20Insights/Drivers%20of%20student%20performance%20Insights%20from%20North%20America/Drivers-of-Student-Performance-Insights-from-North-America.ashx

Calfas, J. (2017, May 11). Do fidget spinners really help with ADHD? Nope, experts say. Money. Time. Retrieved 16 May 2017.

Canadian Paediatric Society. (2017). Screen time and young children: Promoting health and development in a digital world. *Paediatrics & Child Health, 22(8)*, 461–468.

References

Canfield Fisher, D. (1914). *Mothers and children*. New York: H. Holt and Company.

Carr, N. (2008). Is Google making us stupid? What the Internet is doing to our brains. *The Atlantic, 301*(6). Retrieved 6 October 2008, from http://www.theatlantic.com/doc/200807/google

Carson, R. (2011). *The sense of wonder*. Open Road Media.

Chesterton, G. K. (2004). *Orthodoxy*. MT: Kessinger Publishing.

Chesterton, G. K. (2014). *The G. K. Chesterton Collection*. (50 books). London: Catholic Way Publishing.

Chonchaiya, W., & Pruksananonda, C. (2008). Television viewing associates with delayed language development. *Acta Paediatrica, 97(7)*, 977–982.

Christakis, D. A. (2008). The effects of infant media usage: What do we know and what should we learn? *Acta Paediatrica, 98(1)*, 8–16.

Christakis, D. A. (2010). Infant media viewing: First, do no harm. *Pediatric Annals, 39(9)*, 578–582.

Christakis, D. A. (2011). The effects of fast-pace cartoons. *Pediatrics, 128(4)*.

Christakis, D. A., Gilkerson, J., Richards, J. A., Zimmerman, F. J., Garrison, M. M., Xu, D. . . . Yapanel, U. (2009). Audible television and decreased adult words, infant vocalizations, and conversational turns: A population-based study. *Archives of Pediatrics and Adolescent Medicine, 162(5)*, 411–417.

Christakis, D. A., Ramirez, J. S. B., & Ramirez, J. M. (2012). Overstimulation of newborn mice leads to behavioural differences and deficits in cognitive performance. *Scientific Reports, 2*, 546.

Christakis, D. A., Zimmerman, F. J., DiGiuseppe, D. L., & McCarty, C. A. (2004). Early television exposure and subsequent attentional problems in children. *Pediatrics, 111(4)*, 708–713.

Csikszentmihalyi, M. (1975). *Beyond boredom and anxiety: Experiencing flow in work and play*. San Francisco, CA: Jossey-Bass.

de Saint-Exupéry, A. (2000). *The Little Prince* (R. Howard, Trans.). Mariner Books.

Dekker, S., Lee, N. C., Howard-Jones, P., & Jolles, J. (2012). Neuromyths in education: Prevalence and predictors of misconceptions among teachers. *Frontiers in Psychology, 3*, 429.

Deligiannidi, K., & Howard-Jones, P. A. (2015). The neuroscience literacy of teachers in Greece. *Social and Behavioral Sciences, 174,* 3909–3915.

Ednick, M., Cohen, A. P., McPhail, G. L., Beebe, D., Simakajornboon, N., & Amin, R. S. (2009). A review of the effects of sleep during the first year of life on cognitive, psychomotor, and temperament development. *Sleep, 1(32),* 1449–1458.

Engel, S. (2011). Children's need to know: Curiosity in schools. *Harvard Educational Review, 81(4),* 625–645.

Ferrero, M., Garaizar, P., & Vadillo, M. (2016). Neuromyths in education: Prevalence among Spanish teachers and an exploration of cross-cultural variation. *Frontiers in Human Neuroscience, 10,* 496.

Flowers, W. (2007, Oct. 23). *Ceremonia investidura grado honoris causa universidad Andrés Bello Dr. Woodie Flowers* [Dr. Woodie Flowers *honoris causa* investiture ceremony Andrés Bello University]. https://web.archive.org/web/20110929144708/http://www.unab.cl/flowers/descargas/discurso2.pdf

Fulghum, R. cited in Zimmer, B. J. (2003) Reflections for Tending the Sacred Garden. *iUniverse.* 296. P.182.

Garrison, M. M., & Christakis, D. A. (2005). *A teacher in the living room: Educational media for babies, toddlers, and preschoolers.* Menlo Park, CA: The Henry J. Kaiser Family Foundation.

Ginsburg, K. R., American Academy of Pediatrics, Committee on Communications, Committee on Psychosocial Aspects of Child and Family Health. (2007). The importance of play in promoting healthy child development and maintaining strong parent-child bonds. *Pediatrics, 119(1),* 182–191.

Goertzel, M. G., & Goertzel, V. H. (1960). Intellectual and emotional climate in families procuring eminence. *Gifted Child Quarterly, 4,* 59–60.

Goodrich, S. A., Pempek, T. A., & Calvert, S. L. (2009). Formal production features of infant and toddler DVDs. *Archives of Pediatrics & Adolescent Medicine,* 163(12), 1151–1156.

Goswami, U. (2006). Neuroscience and education: From research to practice. *Nature Reviews Neuroscience, 7,* 406–413.

Guardini, R. (1981). La situación incompleta del hombre actual [The incomplete situation of the modern man]. In *Obras Selectas I* [Selected Works I]. Madrid, Spain: Ediciones Cristiandad.

Guardini, R. (1997). *Las etapas de la vida: Su importancia para la ética y la pedagogía*. Biblioteca Plabra.

Hancox, R. J., Milne, B. J., & Poulton, R. (2005). Association of television viewing during childhood with poor educational achievement. *Archives of Pediatrics and Adolescent Medicine, 159(7)*, 614–618.

The Henry J. Kaiser Family Foundation. (2004). *Parents, media and public policy: A Kaiser Family Foundation survey*. Menlo Park, CA.

Honoré, C. (2010). *Under pressure: Putting the child back in childhood*. Knopf Canada.

Howard-Jones, P. (2007). Neuroscience and education: Issues and opportunities, commentary by the Teacher and Learning Research Programme. London: Economic and Social Research Council, TLRP. Retrieved from http://www.tlrp.org/pub/commentaries.html

Howard-Jones, P. A. (2014). Neuroscience and education: Myths and messages. *Nature Reviews Neuroscience, 15*, 817–824.

Huxley, T. H., & Youmans, W. J. (1868). *The elements of physiology and hygiene: A text-book for educational institutions*. New York, NY: Appleton & Co.

Hyatt, K. J. (2007). Brain Gymä building stronger brains or wishful thinking? *Remedial and Special Education, 28(2)*, 117–124.

Infant, preschooler DVDs. (2005, Feb. 14). *Drug Store News, 27(2)*, 38. Retrieved from http://connection.ebscohost.com/c/articles/16139638/infant-preschooler-dvds

Janouch, G. (2012). *Conversations with Kafka (2nd ed.)*. New Directions Publishing.

Jodorowsky, A. (2014). *The Dance of Reality: A Psychomagical Autobiography*. Simon & Schuster.

Johnson, J., Cohen, P., Kasen, S., & Brook, J. S. (2007). Extensive television viewing and the development of attention and learning difficulties during adolescence. *Archives of Pediatrics and Adolescent Medicine, 161(5)*, 480–486.

Kim, K. H. (2011). The creativity crisis: The decrease in creative thinking scores on the Torrance Tests of Creative Thinking. *Creativity Research Journal, 23(4)*, 285–295.

Kirschner, P. A., Sweller, J., & Clark, R. E. (2006). Why minimal guidance during instruction does not work: An analysis of the failure of constructivist, discovery, problem-based, experiential, and inquiry-based teaching. *Journal of Educational Psychology*, 41, 75–86.

Kirschner, P., & De Bruyckere, P. (2017). The myths of the digital native and the multitasker. *Teaching and Teacher Education*. *67*, 135 –142.

Kirsh, S. J., & Mounts, J. R. (2007). Violent video game play impacts facial emotion recognition. *Aggressive Behavior, 33*, 353–358.

Klein-Radukic, S., & Zmyj, N. (2016). The relation between contingency preference and imitation in 6–8-month-old infants. *International Journal of Behavioral Development, 40(2)*, 173–180.

Kübler-Ross, E. (1975). *The Final Stage of Growth*. New York: Scribner.

Kuhl, P. K., Tsao, F. M., & Liu, H. M. (2003). Foreign-language experience in infancy: Effects of short-term exposure and social interaction on phonetic learning. *Proceedings of the National Academy of Sciences of the United States of America, 100(15)*, 9096–9101.

L'Ecuyer, C. (2014). The Wonder Approach to learning. *Frontiers in Human Neuroscience*.

Lerner, C., & Barr, R. (2014). Screen sense: Setting the record straight; Research-based guidelines for screen use for children under 3 years old. *Zero to Three*. Retrieved 11 April 2017 from https://www.zero tothree.org/resources/series/screen-sense-setting-the-record-straight

Linebarger, D. L., & Walker, D. (2005). Infants' and toddlers' television viewing and language outcomes. *American Behavioral Scientist, 48(5)*, 624–645.

Mayer, R. E. (2004). Should there be a three-strikes rule against pure discovery learning? *American Psychologist, 59*, 14–19.

Mendelsohn, A. L., Berkule, S. B., & Tomopoulos, S. (2008). Infant television and video exposure associated with limited parent-child verbal interactions in low socioeconomic status households. *Archives of Pediatrics and Adolescent Medicine, 162(5)*, 411–417.

Montessori, M. (1936). *The secret of childhood*. London: Ballantine Books.

Montessori, M. (1965). *The child in the Church*. E. M. Standing (Ed.). Chantilly, France: Catechetic.

Montessori, M. (1967). *The absorbent mind*. New York, NY: Delta.

References

Montessori, M. (1989). *The child in the family*. The Clio Montessori Series, vol. 8. ABC: CLIO.

Moser, A., Zimmerman, L., Dickerson, K., Grenell, A., Barr, R., & Gerhardstein, P. (2015). They can interact, but can they learn? Toddlers' transfer learning from touchscreens and television. *Journal of Experimental Child Psychology, 137*, 137–155.

Ophir, E., Nass, C., & Wagner, A. D. (2009). Cognitive control in media multitaskers. *Proceedings of the National Academy of Sciences of the United States of America, 106(37)*, 15,583–15,587.

Organization for Economic Co-operation and Development. (2002). *Understanding the brain: Towards a new learning science*. Paris, France: OECD.

Pagani, L. S., Fitzpatrick, C., Barnett, T. A., & Dubow, E. (2010). Prospective associations between early childhood television exposure and academic, psychosocial, and physical well-being by middle childhood. *Archives of Pediatrics and Adolescent Medicine, 164(5)*, 425–431.

Pei, X., Howard-Jones, P. A., Zhang, S., Liu, X., & Jin, Y. (2015). Teachers' understanding about the brain in East China. *Social and Behavioral Sciences, 194*, 3681–3688.

Planck, M. (1932). *Where is science going?* New York, NY: W. W. Norton & Company, Inc.

Postman, N. (2006). *Amusing ourselves to death: Public discourse in the age of show business*. Penguin.

Promethean. (2012). *Educación 3.0, la revista para el aula del siglo XXI* [Education 3.0, the magazine for the 21st century classroom], *6*, 28.

Ra, C. K., Cho, J., Stone, M. D., De La Cerda, J., Goldenson, N. I., Moroney, E., . . . Leventhal, A. M. (2018). Association of Digital Media Use With Subsequent Symptoms of Attention-Deficit/Hyperactivity Disorder Among Adolescents. JAMA, *320(3)*, 255.

Richert, R. A., Robb, M. B., Fender, J. G., & Wartella, E. (2010). Word learning from baby videos. *Archives of Pediatrics & Adolescent Medicine, 164(4)*, 432–437.

Richtel, M. (2011). A Silicon Valley school that doesn't compute. *New York Times* (digital version).

Rowlands, I., Nicholas D., Williams P., Huntington, P., Fieldhouse M., Gunter B., et al. (2008). The Google generation: The information behaviour of the researcher of the future. *Art Libraries Journal*, *35(1)*, 18–21.

Samples, B. (1977) Mind Cycles and Learning. *Phi Delta Kappa International*. 58(9). 689.

Schmitt, M. E., Pempek, T. A., Kirkorian, H. L., Lund, A. F., & Anderson, D. R. (2008). The effect of background television on the toy play behavior of very young children. *Child Development*, *79(4)*, 1137–1151.

Senior, J. (1983). *The Restoration of the Christian Culture*. Ignatius Press.

Siegel, J. D. (1999). *Toward a biology of compassion: Relationships, the brain and the development of mindsight across the lifespan.* Document presented to John Paul II and the Pontifical Council for the Family, Vatican City, December 1999.

Siegel, J. D. (2001). Toward an interpersonal neurobiology of the developing mind: Attachment relationships, "mindsight", and neural integration. *Infant Mental Health Journal*, *22(1–2)*, 67–94.

Singer, J. L. (2002). Cognitive and affective implications of imaginative play in childhood. In M. Lewis (Comp.), *Child and adolescent psychiatry: A comprehensive textbook* (3rd ed., pp. 252–263). Philadelphia, PA: Lippincott Williams & Wilkins.

Swing, E. L., Gentile, D. A., Anderson, C. A., & Walsh, D. A. (2010). Television and video game exposure and the development of attention problems. *Pediatrics*, *126(2)*, 214–221.

Tanimura, M., Okuma, K., & Kyoshima, K. (2007). Television viewing, reduced parental utterance, and delayed speech development in infants and young children. *Archives of Pediatrics and Adolescent Medicine*, *161(6)*, 618–619.

TED. (2011, December 28). *TedxRainier – Dimitri Christakis – Media and children* [Video file]. Retrieved from https://www.youtube.com/watch?v=BoT7qH_uVNo

Tomopoulos, S., Dreyer, B. P., Berkule, S., Fierman, A. H., Brockmeyer, C., & Mendelsohn, A. L. (2010). Infant media exposure and toddler development. *Archives of Pediatrics & Adolescent Medicine*, *164(12)*, 1105–1111.

Touchette, E., Côté, S., Petit, D., Xuecheng, L., Boivin, M., Falissard, B., Montplaisir, J. Y. (2009). Short nighttime sleep-duration and

References

hyperactivity trajectories in early childhood. *Pediatrics, 124(5),* 985–993.

U.S. Department of Health and Human Services. (1999). *Mental health: A report of the surgeon general.* Rockville, MD: Administration National Institute of Mental Health, Department of Health and Human Services, Substance Abuse and Mental Health Services.

U.S. Department of Health and Human Services. (2011). *Head Start impact study.*

Vandewater, E. A., Bickham, D. S., & Lee, J. H. (2006). Time well spent? Relating television use to children's free-time activities. *Pediatrics, 117(2).*

Vandewater, E. A., Bickham, D. S., Lee, J. H., Cummings, H. M., Wartella, E. A., & Rideout, V. J. (2005). When the television is always on: Heavy television exposure and young children's development. *American Behavioral* Scientist, 48(5), 562–577.

Watson, J. B. (1930). *Behaviorism.* Chicago, IL: University of Chicago Press.

Zimmerman, F. J., & Christakis, D. A. (2007). Associations between content types of early media exposure and subsequent attentional problems. *Pediatrics, 120(5),* 986–992.

Zimmerman, F. J., Christakis, D. A., & Meltzoff, A. N. (2007). Associations between media viewing and language development in children under age 2 years. *The Journal of Pediatrics, 151(4),* 364.

Index

Index